The Las Vegas Advisor Guide to Slot Clubs

Other Huntington Press titles:

The Las Vegas Advisor Guide to Slot Clubs

Jeffrey Compton

HUNTINGTON PRESS

The Las Vegas Advisor Guide to Slot Clubs

Published by:
  Huntington Press
  5280 S. Valley View Blvd., Suite B
  Las Vegas, Nevada 89118
  (702) 597-1884 vox
  (702) 597-5208 fax

ISBN 0-929712-75-7

Editors: Anthony Curtis, Deke Castleman
Production and design: Leslie Jackson
Cover photo: Grant Cyphers
Cover design: Leslie Jackson

Printing History
1st edition—November 1995

For William H. Compton, Sr.
my father and best friend

Acknowledgements

Thanks to William and Donna Compton, Rosella Compton, William Compton Jr., Sharon Ball, Chris Axelrod, Joyce Zabell, Ron Stevens, Jeanne Lyons, John Broughton, Marilyn McCullar, Mike Cheselka, Phil McCombs, Judy Skinner, Jim Daigle, Diana Price, and the Arabica and Jitters roundtables for their constant support and enthusiasm. I'm especially grateful to Rex Collins for his good Irish company through much of this adventure.

Special kudos to fellow writer and friend Bob Dancer for surveying the video poker scene throughout southern Nevada. Bob's dream is to write the ultimate video poker book and we will all be better off when his dream comes true.

First books require more attention than should be allowed by law. This one got far more than its share from Deke Castleman, managing editor of Huntington Press. His comments and criticism are always sincere, accurate, and properly laced with humor.

I'm indebted to the many experts who, without charge or even coaxing, passed on their secrets. Special thanks to Stanford Wong, Max Rubin, the Queen of Ku Pon, J.R., Dom and Marilyn, B.G., John Booth, Claire Harris, David Berman, and the Prodigy group. I also appreciate the many inside perspectives and off-the-record comments shared by dozens of slot hosts and other casino folk. You know who you are and I thank you.

Special appreciation goes to Las Vegas' best computer doctor, Matt Doval, for keeping my hardware up and running during this entire process.

And finally, thank you Anthony Curtis, for your trust, your support, your time, your guidance, and your constant demand for the best.

Table of Contents

Foreword

by Anthony Curtis

Ten years ago, I walked into the Mint (now the Horseshoe) and noticed strings of tickets—the kind you see at skee-ball arcades—hanging from boxes attached to the slot machines and littering the floor. Looking around, I also noticed that most of the casino patrons, even the slot players themselves, were oblivious to them. I harvested the discards and took them to the slot club booth, where I learned that they were worth 25¢ each. And so my first experience with slot clubs left me with the impression that profiting from them could be as easy as picking money up off the floor.

Slot clubs caught on quickly, and by the early 1990s dozens of casinos in Las Vegas had them. Subscribers to my *Las Vegas Advisor* newsletter began writing in with stories of big comp scores attributable to slot club membership. One stayed ten nights in Las Vegas casinos absolutely free. Another racked up 18 nights for a total lodging bill of just $60.

The greatest haul of all was pulled down by a slot club expert who's now known to the world as the Queen of Ku Pon (the nickname she used in a nationally televised "48 Hours" segment that featured her). The Queen—in real life a retired teacher from Indianapolis—was able to stay free in Las Vegas casinos for 49 nights of a 50-night visit (including New Year's Eve and the Super Bowl) because of her numerous slot club affiliations.

My personal slot club epiphany came on a Thursday evening in 1992. As happens sooner or later to anyone who lives in Las Vegas, I found out that a flock of relatives was flying into town for a spur-of-the-moment getaway. They wanted two rooms at the Frontier (where they'd experienced some good fortune on previous trips). I called Frontier reservations and was told that the hotel was "booked solid." By chance, I glimpsed a Frontier slot club card sitting in a pile of things near the phone.

"Well, I'm a slot club member," I said.

"Oh, that makes a difference," the reservations agent responded. She then proceeded to book two rooms for three nights each, and even comped half the bill. What amazed me was that my club account had only limited play, perhaps a few hundred dollars worth of action.

During the past five years, slot club opportunities and strategies have been a primary focus of the *Las Vegas Advisor*, and several proposals for slot club books have crossed my desk, some from capable gamblers (and writers). None of the candidates, though, possessed the critical combination of resources necessary to pull it off—time, energy, and most importantly, capital.

Then Jeffrey Compton showed up. Not only did Jeff possess all three requisite resources, he had something extra—he'd already experienced everything he proposed to write about. Like the authors of all the best gambling and casino-related books, Jeff writes directly from first-hand involvement. He practices everything he preaches on a regular basis; the only thing he did differently to complete this book was turn up the intensity. Jeff visited and revisited the casinos, experimented with redemption options, and interviewed representatives from every club in southern Nevada. The result is the definitive work on the subject.

I'm often asked to identify the casual player's best shot at beating the casinos. The answer is slot clubs, and now the *Las Vegas Advisor Guide to Slot Clubs* provides more useful information on how to profit from them than any other source, anywhere. Don't expect riches, but if you combine the knowledge you glean from within these pages with the tricks you'll learn on your own, you'll find that accruing the benefits—cash, comps, and VIP treatment— is easy. As easy as picking money up off the floor.

Introduction

This book was born from hunger.

When I relocated to Las Vegas, I had recently sold a small manufacturing business to a long-time employee and had a tidy little guaranteed income. With careful budgeting and proper investing, I would be able to live well into the next decade with few financial worries, as long as I ate at home. That was the rub. I love to eat out, and I hadn't moved to Las Vegas, the world's greatest 24-hour dining room, to miss out on my favorite pastime. On the other hand, I couldn't afford a $500-per-month meals and entertainment budget, either.

Some Las Vegas residents and tourists obtain free meals via casino complimentaries, or comps, as they're known. That was not a viable alternative for me. I have trouble totaling more than three cards in blackjack. I'm allergic to dogs and horses and am bored by sports. I lose track of crap bets, and if I have two pair or better, I somehow find a way to tell everyone at the poker table. Given my limitations playing the traditional gambling games, I assumed that I would have to lose $1,000 to qualify for a $5.95 buffet.

I do enjoy playing video poker, though—nothing complicated, just jacks or better. One day about three months after I moved here, a neighbor told me that he and his wife get several free meals and line passes (allowing them to bypass the line) at the Golden Nugget, thanks to their membership in the casino's 24 Karat Slot Club. What's the catch, I wanted to know. I was told you had to be a full member of the club, which meant earning 150 slot club points (in layman's terms, play a total of $2,250 in a slot or video poker machine). Since I was planning to play dollar video poker that weekend anyway, I thought I'd play at the Golden Nugget and see if I could earn the points before my money (about $300) ran out.

That Friday night, I drove downtown, walked into the casino, joined the 24 Karat Club, and hit the machines. After an hour of playing 9/6 jacks or better video poker, I was down about $25, but I also had four beers under my belt, a $15 rebate check in my wallet, and a comp for two buffets. What's more, I was a VIP at a glamorous Las Vegas resort!

Bolstered by my good fortune, I decided to see how many slot clubs I could join by the end of what was to become a fateful lost weekend. Within three days, I was a member of the privileged set at The Mirage, Excalibur, Caesars Palace, and the Las Vegas Hilton. I filled out applications at several other casinos that didn't require pre-membership play and added their cards to my colorful new collection.

At first, I considered that weekend an isolated adventure, but I soon found out that I had started something big. My mailbox began filling up with offers for free meals, two-for-one coupons, and other inducements from casinos whose cards I'd acquired. I took advantage of some of those offers and continued to use my club cards when I played, and it wasn't long before I realized that my normal level of video poker play was yielding an additional bonus of at least two free meals per week. Not only had I stumbled upon a solution to my "eating disorder," I'd also found a cheap way to entertain (and impress) the steady stream of visitors that had seemingly followed me from the midwest to my new home.

When you live in Las Vegas, you entertain guests. Lots of guests. With 30 million people visiting Las Vegas every year, sooner or later everyone you know and everyone they know will pass through your life.

Here's an example. Christmas week, I was deluged by a torrent of visitors: one father, one brother, and several friends. Worse, they gave me little notice, so I had no reservations for anything.

Christmas morning, my brother decided that it would be great if we could all go to The Mirage champagne buffet. Being that it was both a Sunday and a holiday, we'd have normally been subjected to a minimum two-hour wait in line. My father is eighty and he didn't like long lines when he was twenty. No problem. Club Mirage was one of the first slot clubs I joined and I've been an active member ever since. On our way into the casino, I stopped by the slot club booth and asked for three line passes. After checking my account, The Mirage's ever-efficient slot hosts not only issued the passes, but comped two of the buffets as well. We walked to the front of a line of at least a hundred people, many of whom pull a lot more levers than I do. While they waited, we ate like three kings (wisemen?) for two hours—for less than $15.

On the way home, my father noticed that Harry Blackstone Jr. was performing at Bally's. Being a big fan of the Blackstones, both Jr. and Sr., he offered to treat if I could get tickets. Small problem. Blackstone shows up only once a year and always sells out. Though I was a member of Bally's MVP Slot Club, I had very few comp points in that account. Regardless, I called the special club phone number and asked if they could handle this same-day order. The show's entire run had been sold out, but there were some last-minute cancellations in the high-roller area. We got seats right next to the stage. Blackstone disappeared twice right before my father's eyes and he is still talking about it. Yes, we were lucky the cancellations materialized, but without the slot club connection we would have had no chance.

New Year's Eve at 9:30 p.m., two friends and I decided to ring out the old at Treasure Island. We arrived to find NBC televising the Las Vegas segment of its New Year's Eve telecast in front of the hotel. A throng of thousands milled around in the street and the casino was closed to all but hotel guests and VIPs. No problem. I whipped out my Treasure Island Club card and three more VIPs were admitted. We headed straight for the Battle Bar. I showed my card to the doorman and he showed us to three seats overlooking Buccaneer Bay, a couple of life-sized sailing ships, lots of fireworks, and 50,000 revelers.

As you can see, slot clubs can help make holidays special, but they also come in handy the rest of the year. How? My personal benefit list is full of the following.

Cash—Depending on the casino, I receive rebates ranging from 9¢ to $1 for every $100 that I play. Often that rebate gives me a mathematical edge in the game. For example, if I'm playing a full-pay jacks or better video poker machine at the Golden Nugget, my theoretical payback is $100.17 for every $100 I gamble.

Meal comps—In theory, I average one meal comp per every two hours of quarter slot play. In reality, I put on 15 pounds last year and I can't remember the last time I paid for a meal in a casino.

Casino rate—If I need a room I pay, at worst, half what the average visitor pays at any hotel. At best, I get the room for free.

Entertainment comps—Caesars Palace regularly sends me offers for two free tickets to its headliner shows, including David Copperfield and Jerry Seinfeld. If a casino is launching a new production, such as *EFX* at MGM Grand, I can expect free weekday tickets or a 50% discount.

Priority treatment—As a casino VIP, I'm given special handling for any meal, room, or show reservation I need. If the event is sold out, I can still usually get a ticket or two, and if sales are slow, the club will sometimes offer tickets for free. I have even used the club to secure room reservations on busy weekends for out-of-town friends, a cherished perk that tends to keep my house a lot less crowded.

Gifts—My recent 40th birthday brought forth a plentiful bounty: a Caesars Palace sweatshirt, $100 free play on The Mirage Megabucks machine, several meals (including two at Sam's Town's new steakhouse), a roll of quarters, two Fiesta drinking mugs, and a free weekend stay complete with meals at the Hacienda. I'd wager that I'm the only person in my high school class who can't wait until his next birthday!

Unlimited buffet line passes—I have a standing deal with my friends: I get us to the front of the line and they pay for the meal.

Invitations—I'm on the A-list for New Year's Eve, the Super Bowl, and celebrations to open a new casino or to blow up the one next door.

The list goes on and on....

At press time, there are more than forty different slot clubs in Las Vegas, and that doesn't include Laughlin, Mesquite, and Jean. Most offer cash, comps, and other benefits, along with friendly folks in the slot club booth to fully explain the rules and dispense the goodies. A few offer little more than a hassle and a headache. Whether you play nickels, quarters, dollars, or five dollars, slots or video poker, there is a slot club in southern Nevada for you. Finding the best fit requires homework, footwork, and capital. This book allows you to make the minimum investment of all three.

The information in *The Las Vegas Advisor Guide to Slot Clubs* was gathered first-hand, checked, and rechecked. Bob Dancer (a first-rate video poker player and key collaborator on this book) and I visited every casino in southern Nevada. I signed up for every slot club that existed and fulfilled the requirements needed to become a permanent or at least an active member. During most of my gambling sessions I broke even, though on occasion I lost enough to treat the entire slot club staff to the buffet. Ultimately, a large jackpot at The Mirage (thank you, Mr. Wynn) enabled me to complete this project in the black (and pay for my new patio).

Thanks to slot clubs I got my ultimate wish. I am able to eat out whenever I want, see first-rate entertainment, and occasionally add a few dollars to my budget.

You can, too.

The Short History
of Slot Clubs

Slot clubs were born in Atlantic City, New Jersey. What, not Las Vegas? No, Atlantic City. Ever since the first casino opened there in 1978, Atlantic City has attracted a very different clientele than her more glamorous older sister—not high-rolling table-game players or subsidized conventioneers or even three-day weekenders, but cost-conscious day-trippers who primarily play quarter slot machines. With ten casinos nestled on the boardwalk, one indistinguishable from the next, each property recognized that its bread-and-butter customers had to be induced to stay and play, or they'd walk next door.

In 1982, the Sands Casino issued an executive-committee directive to its slot department manager to "create a plan that recognizes slot players as appreciated customers." Four weeks later the Galaxy Slot Club debuted. Floor personnel and other casino staff were told to look for familiar faces, even if they played nickels, and get their names and addresses. The selected customers were invited to special parties and given gold lapel pins to help identify them as casino VIPs. After its first year, the Galaxy Slot Club had 600 members and was considered to be an overwhelming success.

In 1983, Harrah's Atlantic City expanded on the concept. Borrowing directly from the airlines' frequent-flyer programs, Harrah's devised a system whereby players received one ticket (a sort of bonus buck) for every hundred dollars or so they put through the slot machines. Players could redeem their tickets in the hotel restaurants and gift shops or apply them to their hotel bills.

In 1984, Steve Wynn, who at the time owned the Golden Nugget in Atlantic City, brought slot clubs to Las Vegas. He inaugurated the 24 Karat Club at the Golden Nugget which, as in Atlantic City, employed ticket dispensers located next to slot machines. Each time the machine was played the dispenser would "count down" a particular monetary amount. When the counter hit zero, a ticket was dispensed.

The Golden Nugget 24 Karat Club is also responsible for introducing another enduring concept (though not intentionally) to Las Vegas: direct cash rebates to slot players. The first brochure about Las Vegas' first slot club stated that members could apply tickets toward the cost of anything in the hotel—including additional dollar tokens. The casino soon saw the allure of the cash rebate and made it the focus of future advertising. Several Las Vegas casinos, particularly in the downtown area, followed suit.

Though the slot club concept showed immediate promise, much of the industry took a decidedly wait-and-see attitude, especially toward cash rebates. Providing ways for players to walk out the door with money has never appealed to casino owners. But like all things in Las Vegas, competition and the changing market dictated the evolution and ultimate acceptance of slot clubs. As more and more casino space was devoted to slots, more and more casino ex-

THE "NO SLOT CLUB"...

In late 1990, Palace Station (and its parent company Station Casinos) launched a still-famous marketing campaign to attract slot players by advertising that it did not have a slot club. With headlines like "No Slot Club Means Bigger Jackpots," the ads suggested that because Palace Station did not have to spend money on prizes and operational expenses, it could pay out more to slot players. One memorable ad depicted a caricature of George Bush under the headline, "Read my lips! No new taxes! Slot clubs are free!"

According to unverified industry gossip, Palace Station was on the verge of starting a club when it ran into equipment problems. The marketing department came up with the "No Slot Club" campaign as a way out of the morass.

Like most marketing ideas, this one was not new. Thirty years ago in my Ohio hometown, a particular grocer frequently advertised that he could offer lower prices because his store did not hand out trading stamps. As I remember, soda pop and candy bars (the only things I bought back then) cost the same in that store as anywhere else.

ecutives, especially younger computer-literate MBAs, realized the value of knowing who their slot players were and how to keep them happy.

In the late 1980s, the casinos began attaching ATM-like devices to (and later installed them right into) their slot machines, handing out personalized plastic cards to club members, and relying on computers to manage the growing databases of information. These developments represented more than just a technological advance. They also heralded a huge conceptual leap in the casino's use of slot clubs as a marketing tool. The new "player tracking systems" didn't just tabulate the kind of action slot club members were generating. They were also capable of making demographic data accessible on demand, identifying gambling patterns, and even alerting the slot control room when there was heavy slot action by a non-member (no card inserted), thus enabling the club staff to sign up a new recruit.

The next step was to expand computerized player tracking beyond just slots to include table games. Bingo, keno, and sports bet-

...DEBATE ENDS

Several studies, including one by the *Las Vegas Advisor*, revealed that the same thing was true at Palace Station. Though slot machine return percentages could not be compared, video poker returns could, and Palace Station's video poker return was no better than any of the other casinos catering to locals.

The competition's response to the "No Slot Club" campaign was equally memorable. A full-page Gold Coast ad shouted "Don't be railroaded," while a similar Sam's Town piece displayed a smoke-spewing locomotive above the headline, "Don't get caught in the smoke screen."

Station Casinos is currently installing card readers on every slot machine in Palace and Boulder Stations. The machines at Texas, its newest casino, had readers already built in before the casino opened. But every time you use the words "slot club" there, booth personnel correct you, insisting that you refer to it as a "player tracking system." One manager told me that "It has became obvious to us that players' opinions on slot clubs have changed over the last five years." I agree that someone's mind has changed, but I think it's the casino's.

ting followed. Now the ability to track and reward all casino customers (not just high rollers) existed.

Though slot clubs are just a decade old in Las Vegas, their future is assured. All the megaresorts that have opened in the last six years had their slot clubs up and running on opening day. Even the old green-felt war horses on the Strip, which looked down on "two-bit bettors" just a few years ago, have joined the fold. The few remaining holdouts either have less than 500 slot machines and cannot justify the expense, or choose to employ other methods to attract players, such as running periodic promotions or monitoring player coin purchases.

The innovations keep coming. Most recently, Harrah's Las Vegas introduced several computerized comp machines (another Atlantic City import) so slot and table players can write their own meal ticket without having to visit the Gold Card booth or talk to a host.

Thirteen years ago, the Sands in Atlantic City boasted 600 members. Today, Las Vegas' largest slot club at the Gold Coast casino claims more than 300,000! With the city's hotel-room inventory approaching 100,000 and annual visitations on the verge of exceeding 30 million, there is no end in sight.

2

Why Slot Clubs?

S lot clubs can be found throughout Nevada, in Atlantic City, on Mississippi riverboats, and at Indian casinos across America. In Las Vegas, new clubs have been recently introduced at the Hard Rock, Imperial Palace, Rio, Desert Inn, and Texas. Though New York-New York, the megaresort under construction at Tropicana and the Strip, will not open until December 1996, the on-site visitors center is already collecting names. Why? Because an effective slot club is a win-win for both the casino and the player.

CASINO GOALS

Establishing a slot club is no easy task. According to an executive at Fitzgeralds, which is just instituting a system, the up-front costs including card readers, computers, printers, installation labor, and staff training can easily run more than a million dollars. Then there's annual upkeep, which includes labor (slot hosts, slot booth personnel, supervisors, maintenance), new and replacement equipment, marketing and advertising, and let's not forget the prizes—cash, comps, and merchandise.

So why do casinos have slot clubs? To attract, reward, and ultimately retain slot players. They might not be as sexy as baccarat players, but there are a lot more of them and they're far more desirable. Slot clubs require staff, but slot machines don't, thus the casino can avoid additional personnel and the attending costs: salaries, benefits, occasional incompetence, personal hassles, even theft. Also, slot players require no training or prior experiences to be able to begin gambling (unlike table-game players), and a "loose" 98% return machine cannot be beaten over the long run, even when the slot club kicks back an additional 1%.

Unfortunately for the casinos, slot players' loyalties can be fleeting. Since slot machines do not vary much from casino to casino, a losing session can easily send a player scurrying across the street to find better machines. Also, there's little personal contact with the casino employees, so relationships and allegiances aren't formed. Slot players usually wind up going back to the place where they won the most money on their last trip. The only way to combat these negatives is to identify and evaluate desired players, then entice them to come back.

Prior to automated slot clubs, many casinos rewarded slot players based on the highly subjective judgment of a change person or host who had observed the player in action for a short time (as they do on table games). Since slot-area personnel have many more players to service than their table-game counterparts, savvy players knew when to play fast (they were being watched) or slow (they weren't). Gamblers also knew the power of giving generous tips to minimum-wage help.

Today's new breed of casino manager prefers using computers (over hiring additional employees) for tracking slot play and administering comps. The advantages are many. Computers can't be toked, so bribery is out. With regard to tabulating the total amount of money bet, computers can't be tricked. But the major advantage of a computer is the amount of information it can collect, sort, and disburse.

Be aware that when you join and use a slot club, you're giving the casino much more information than just your name, address, social security number, and birthday. You also give it the means to determine what and how you play, how long and how often you play, and what rewards you're playing for. Entire marketing departments, complete with database engineers and direct-mail coordinators, are created to maximize the value of this information.

ADVANTAGE TO THE PLAYER

Okay, now we know why casinos have slot clubs, but what's in it for the player? Lots of things, as we'll soon see, but the main advantage can be summed up in two words: ties win.

In a recent article for *Casino Player*, Anthony Curtis wrote that the creators of video poker did something that no other gambling-game developer has ever been able to do: they made a push (tie) seem like a win. A pair of jacks, queens, kings, or aces returns your original wager. Even though it's a push, it feels like a profit. He's right.

But when you belong to a slot club, a push *is* a profit. That's because every coin you send through a machine counts toward something of value later on.

Statistically, a jacks or better video poker player will lose 54%

of the hands he plays, win 25%, and tie the remaining 21%. Since slot clubs turn ties into wins, the slot club member comes out ahead almost twice as often as the non-member.

True, the win is minuscule if there is only one play, but after a weekend of gambling (or 4,000 plays), the slot club benefits become a (or the) major factor in the player's overall win or loss.

An example: Two people are playing quarter slots. After eight hours of action, both are even; neither has won nor lost any money. Player A, the slot club member, walks away with $40, two free meals and $50 credited off her hotel bill. Player B gets nothing.

They both tied, but who won?

Let's take the concept further. I play a three-coin $1 slot machine with a 97% return for eight hours at Caesars Palace. Assuming I play 500 hands per hour, I would be betting a total of $1,500 an hour or $12,000 for the entire period of play. My theoretical loss is $360 dollars, but as an Emperors Club member, I get an $80 cash rebate, $60 in free meals, and $60 knocked off my room charge. This effectively reduces my loss by $200.

Now for a really fun example. You play quarter bonus deuces at Sam's Town for eight hours. Assuming you've studied the game and play near perfectly, your theoretical win is about 1% of your entire action ($1.25 x 600 hands per hour x 8 hours), or $60. That's not bad. Now add the $6 slot club rebate and a meal comp for $40 and it's even better. Five hours of play and you've earned $106.

When you join a slot club, you're guaranteed to at least get something for your time pushing buttons (or pulling levers). It may not equal what you lose playing the machine, but frequently, especially if you play sharp video poker, the slot club rebate will turn a losing session into a winning one.

KNOWLEDGE IS POWER

Whenever you give up information about yourself, you're assisting the casino. Management puts that information to work designing promotions, slot areas, and even entire casinos which they hope, in the long run, will work to separate you from your money.

Two can play that game. Where gambling, casinos, and slot clubs are concerned, the more you know, the further you'll go.

There are more than 40 slot clubs in Las Vegas, which means that there are more than 40 different marketing strategies used to attract members, because no two clubs work exactly alike. They vary in the type of rewards they give, how large the rewards are, and the rules that govern how the rewards are disbursed. Every club has its idiosyncrasies and subtleties, and these frequently create benefits that even the staff isn't aware of. The only aspect that they all have in common is that the more you know about any or all of them, the more rewards you will take home. By learning about the various club systems and reward schemes, a sharp member can guarantee he'll give up a great deal less than he gains.

Throughout this book, I urge you to create a personal "ABC" system, which you can use to categorize the various clubs.

"C" clubs are clubs that you simply join. Since you will join every club, no slot club can be less than a C. The only exception would be a club with pre-membership play requirements that are beyond your normal gambling comfort zone (Mirage, Golden Nugget).

"B" clubs are those that you'll use, a least a little, because you have one or two good reasons for playing in that casino, such as maintaining your casino-rate qualification. I don't play at the Barbary Coast except during bonus-point periods. My goal is to secure enough points to earn a dinner comp at Michael's, its ultra-wonderful gourmet room.

"A" clubs are your gems. You will work these cards hard. These are the clubs located at the casinos you enjoy playing, eating, and sleeping at. They have your favorite machines, and the rewards are things that are valuable to you. Before long, you'll know everything there is to know about the reward system, you'll be friends with one or two of the key personnel, and you'll know each and every angle imaginable.

DON'T ASK, WON'T TELL

Within the casino universe are a pocket of clubs that want to know everything about you, but don't want you to know anything about them. Some of them insist on calling themselves "player tracking systems" as opposed to slot clubs. My nickname for these clubs is "don't ask, won't tell."

These secretive systems can usually be distinguished by three attributes: the club awards comps and not cash; player cards can be used throughout the casino including slots, video poker, table games, keno, bingo, and the sports book; and most importantly, the system tells the players very little about what comps they have accrued and what is required to earn more. Many of these systems don't have the common courtesy to call you by name. You insert your card in the reader, which says "Card Accepted" and little else.

Casinos that take the route of secretive player tracking are motivated by fear and control. Though the casino wants to partake of the business benefits the slot club provides, its top executives want to avoid the threat of exploitation (usually by highly skilled video poker players). They want complete control over who gets the goodies under their roof.

In my opinion, these new slot clubs (excuse me, player-tracking systems) will eventually discover that two others factors also affect the situation: service and competition. When a casino introduces a system where the player has to ask about every little detail, the operation needs additional personnel to handle the inquiries. And the personnel need to be courteous, well-informed, and professionally trained in customer relations, or they'll run off the casino's steady slot customers. They'd better also be well paid, because they'll be standing on the firing line day in and day out answering all the questions that the secretive system creates. In other words, secrecy does not come cheap.

On the other hand, competition (the consumer's true best friend) has precipitated the emergence of cash rebates in more than 50% of the clubs, including all the megaresorts and several recent downtown converts. The few attempts to eliminate cash rebates resulted in such serious player resistance that the casinos either reverted back (the Sands in 1991) or went into comp overdrive to make up the difference (the Frontier). A more common defense is for the casino to slowly eliminate the higher paying video poker machines. This strategy is infinitely easier in Strip casinos than in those catering to the tougher local trade.

The casino slot club drama—the desire to control versus the necessity to compete—is being played out all over southern Nevada. It should remain quite fascinating for years to come. Ultimately, the issue may be settled when the members vote with their feet, walking away from the secretive systems and into the user-friendly cash-rebate clubs.

3

Flipping the Switch—
Joining Slot Clubs

Raise your right hand and repeat after me: *I will join every slot club at every casino I visit. I will not deposit my hard-earned money into any slot or video poker machine unless I belong to that slot club. I will always use my slot club card even if I deposit a single quarter.*

Why should you join every slot club? Because you have nothing to lose and literally everything to gain. Many clubs give free gifts or discount coupons to anyone who fills out the form. Casino shops and restaurants frequently offer 10%-15% discounts to card-carrying members. A month from now you could receive offers for discounted rooms or food. But first you have to join.

That said, let's walk though the joining process. You've arrived at the TNT Casino. Whether you're staying there, you just walked in off the Strip, or someone recommended it, your mission is to join, gather as much data as possible, then add it to your A, B, or C list.

First, check the slot and video poker machines. Does the casino offer a selection of the machines you like to play at a denomination you are comfortable with? Do those machines have card readers? Look closely to make sure you're not mistaking the device used for accepting (and usually rejecting) paper money for a card reader. If the machines have card readers, the casino probably offers slot club benefits for play at that denomination. (There are exceptions. Treasure Island, for example, has slot club card readers on its quarter slots even though they are not used. Maybe accepting measly quarters is in its long-term plan.)

Even if the machines don't have card readers, the joint may still have some form of slot promotions or incentives, such as "bonus buck" programs, so be sure to ask a slot host about it. (Slot hosts are employed by the casino to host slot players. They are usually on the casino floor greeting players, writing comps, taking pictures of jackpot winners, and generally being helpful and friendly. See Chapter Six for a full discussion of the proper care and feeding of slot hosts.)

Just before going to the booth to sign up, look around the casino to see if it stocks any weekly freebie magazines. The freebies (along with the local daily newspapers) are the best place to learn about any special enticements or bonuses the casino might be running to get new members to join the club (and, if possible, should be checked out before your daily slot club search). Various clubs offer bonus points, two-for-one food coupons, even cash to anyone presenting a special coupon upon sign-up. Also check the casino funbook, where you might find a coupon for bonus points or other incentives to join.

THE APPLICATION FORM

Now it's time to find the slot club booth, usually located at the rear of the casino next to the cashier. If you can't find it, ask a change person or other casino employee where it is.

Fill out the application (legibly), supplying your name, address, birthday, and (sometimes) your social security number. You may also be asked to produce picture identification, such as a driver's license. Most clubs require photo identification when you sign up and all require it when you redeem your points for a prize, especially cash. This is done for several reasons, including player verification and compliance with state gaming regulations and federal tax law.

The form usually has a place for you to identify your gambling preferences, hobbies, and interests, such as slot tournaments, sports betting, bingo, etc. In order to be included in as many special mailings as possible, check off any and all boxes that even mildly interest you.

One of the questions on the form asks if you are married and what your spouse's name is. Let's pause here.

If you're single, nothing prevents you from listing a fictitious spouse and wedding date. The casino won't go to the trouble to verify this, and you might get another batch of goodies on your "anniversary." (Keep in mind, however, if you do get married, you might have some explaining to do!)

If you really are married, it may be best to maintain separate accounts, as opposed to a joint account. This way, if a special weekend package is mailed to all southern California members, for example, the household gets two weekends instead of one. If you take my advice and sign up separately, you should show up at the booth separately, preferably on different days.

If you don't plan to run more than $500 each per trip through the machines at that casino, you're probably better off combining your points into one account. Casinos rarely reward action that adds up to less than $1,000 per day. (Note: The terms "action" and "play" refer to the total amount of money deposited into a slot machine, not how much you win or lose. The average quarter player generates $625-$750 worth of action per hour; dollar players run through $2,500-$3,000 per hour.)

Either way, always ask for two cards. All clubs allow you and your spouse to run up points together on two different machines. If you're single, you're usually allowed to have a friend run up points on your duplicate card if both of you are in the casino at the same time.

THE PERSONNEL

While signing up, be observant of booth personnel. Are they intelligent and accommodating, eager to answer all your questions and make you feel welcome? Or are they merely keypunching your card and rattling off a routine, oblivious to your specific concerns? The quality and professionalism of slot booth personnel directly reflect the importance placed on the entire slot club operation by casino management. This observation is important in terms of rating the slot club on A, B, or C lists.

What kind of questions should you ask? All kinds. Ask how points are accumulated at your level (nickels, quarters, dollars, etc.) and game (slots, video poker, video keno, video blackjack). Many clubs do not include nickel play and a few don't count quarters. Several clubs award more points for slots than they do for video poker.

Ask if the club awards cash or prizes. If it awards cash, ascertain how many points are needed to win $1 (see page 39). If prizes and comps are the main awards, ask to see a prize schedule. Though you don't have to evaluate this information completely before you sign up, you should definitely work through it before you begin serious play.

Some slot clubs, such as those run by Circus Circus and The Mirage, are forthcoming with information; their personnel take as much time as necessary to answer all your questions. At the other extreme are the "don't ask, won't tell" clubs, such as the Aladdin, Tropicana, and Hard Rock, that would have you believe there is no way for them to determine what the point schemes are or how many points you need to get a free meal or reduced room rate. Don't believe this for a second! They could tell you if they wanted to. The long-term trend in Las Vegas has been to disclose more and more information to members. This trend is pressuring some secretive clubs to rethink their policies. You can support this movement by refusing to play at the ones that insist on a "don't ask, won't tell" stance.

THE ACTIVATION POINT

While you're at the booth, take a moment to check "activation points." In order to separate the players from the joiners, most clubs require a minimum level of action, to reach what's called the activation point, before they'll give you any serious benefits or discounts.

The majority of slot clubs issue you one or two cards and any other sign-up bonuses right on the spot. Your vital statistics go into their databases and you're immediately eligible to receive special offers in the mail. (Tip: To guarantee this minimum-level treatment, you should plan on putting at least $100 worth of action on the card after each sign-up. But you won't really be considered a VIP until you've reached and surpassed the activation point.)

Many of the higher-paying cash clubs, such as Club Mirage, establish this hurdle upon sign-up by issuing you a temporary card, but not granting full membership until after you've run a specified amount (about $2,500) through their machines. A fast dollar slot player should be able to do this in an hour. Once accomplished, you're given a check (about $10-$15) and, more importantly, VIP status that entitles you to a special room discount (casino rate), along with some nifty T-shirts. Qualifying time periods vary. Some clubs give you up to a year to earn the required points; others, such as Excalibur, have a seven-day limit.

Some clubs are less forthcoming about activation points. Much depends on whether you live in that casino's target market. Strip casinos, as well as the larger downtown operations, cater primarily to out-of-towners, while the outlier joints on Boulder Highway or Rancho Boulevard are looking for locals. Those players who live in the target market will be able to activate their memberships sooner, i.e., receive more for less action.

The best way to estimate the activation point is to ask booth personnel if they have a newsletter and how many points are required to receive it. In lieu of that, several other important demarcation points can be identified. You can inquire about the point levels required to obtain a free T-shirt, the minimum cash rebate, or the casino rate on a room. If your bankroll can handle it, you should try to reach the activation point if this casino is a candidate for your A or B list.

The Showboat, Lady Luck, Frontier, and several Laughlin casinos have tiered membership levels that deliver rewards in varying degrees based on total lifetime points. Membership tiers and comp levels aren't new concepts, and many casinos use them, but the Lady Luck et al., as part of the trend toward divulging more information, have made the criteria available to members.

WHAT IF MY FAVORITE CASINO DOESN'T HAVE A SLOT CLUB?

Someday, somewhere, you may find yourself in a casino that doesn't have a slot club. It may be the casino closest to your home. The same casino that has special blackjack or crap rules, your favorite restaurant, and your spouse's favorite sports book. Don't despair. Almost every casino with 400 or more slot machines has devised some method to reward their players. The best way to find out is to ask a slot host or supervisor.

Though non-slot club reward systems vary greatly, here is a short list of what to be on the lookout for.

Periodic promotions—Some of the smaller casinos prefer to offer their players limited-time special promotions as opposed to an on-going slot club. Not only is this strategy cheaper, but it allows the casino to adjust its marketing to seasonal swings, economic conditions, or to entice a specific group of customers through the door.

Vacation Village (located at the south end of Las Vegas Blvd. near the airport and the impressive Belz Factory Outlet Mall) is the innovative leader in periodic promotions. It's always running some form of video poker special, such as paying double for certain hands, or passing out bonus bucks when a player gets any four of a kind, or allowing a free spin on a high-paying money wheel. Many expert local players have managed to combine several simultaneous Vacation Village promotions with the full-paying machines (such as 10/7 double bonus) to take home a tidy profit.

So much for locals. For tourists, Vacation Village recently offered anyone who presented a valid airline ticket within twelve hours of arrival a spin on the money wheel. The top prize was complete reimbursement of airfare up to $400 dollars. Another great promotion at this casino has been a complimentary hot dog and beer, for a $10 nickel buy-in at the bar.

If Vacation Village happens to be on the wrong side of town, check out the promotions at Arizona Charlie's in northwest Las Vegas or Binion's Horseshoe downtown.

Paycheck cashing—Most of the local joints, including Arizona Charlie's, Palace Station, and almost any casino in Henderson, will give local players some reward for cashing their paychecks there. This can vary from a free spin on a giveaway wheel to special bonuses for video poker. Your employer must be on an approved list before the casino will accept the check. Though it is possible to double your paycheck, it's also possible to gamble away the rent money. Strong of will only, please.

Super nickel play—An argument could be made that nickel players should not be concerned about slot clubs, but should be looking instead for high-paying video poker machines. At the various Jackie Gaughan properties, including the Plaza and the El Cortez, you will find excellent video poker nickel machines including 9/6-4700 jacks. Most places that allow nickel play in their slot club do not offer anything close.

4

Piling Up Points

Armed with your new slot club card, you venture out into the casino to find your favorite slot or video poker machine. Based on the knowledge gleaned from the staff at the booth, you've resolved to play enough to reach the activation point.

Once you've decided on a machine, insert your card into the small card reader. The insertion slots may be found in front, on the side, or on top of the machine.

Make sure the card reader is recording the play under your name. You should be greeted by the readout with something like "Hello [Your Name]." If you have a temporary card, the reader will say "Hello Player," or possibly something indigenous, such as at Treasure Island where the card reader says, "Ahoy Player." A secretive system, such as those discussed in Chapter 2, usually says nothing but "Card Accepted." Some casinos, particularly the Barbary Coast and Frontier, and Pioneer in Laughlin, are notorious for malfunctioning equipment, usually due to poor maintenance. I once played a half hour at the Barbary Coast before realizing that the card reader was congratulating "Cheryl" and not "Jeffrey" on earning points. I had to complain loud and long before they made an adjustment to my point total.

Max Rubin's *Comp City* (Huntington Press) recommends that you insert a second card (remember I said always ask for two) in the machine next to yours and play until you've earned some points on both machines. Then stick to playing only one machine, in the process "forgetting" to remove your card from the other. With luck a non-member will come along and play it, thus giving you points for free. If you're like me and always seem to get caught at stuff like this, forget it. If not, this trick is pretty easy to pull off and, if necessary, explain away. (Some dauntless souls will even leave one or both cards in the machines after they finish playing.)

Lost your card or left it at home? Don't worry. All that can happen (if it's lost) is somebody runs up points on your account. They cannot redeem your points because identification is required at redemption. And you can always get a duplicate card from the slot desk without a hassle (except at the Gold Coast where, for some reason, a two-week notice is required before the club will issue a new card). I have as many as seven cards from a single casino, due to the many times I've walked in without one.

TALLYING POINTS

After the greeting, some sort of information will follow. Depending on the club, you might be told how many total unredeemed points you have in your account, how many you've earned so far in the current session, and the "countdown." The countdown is the number of plays, or coins, needed to earn the next point. The countdown could be anywhere from 1 to 360 coins (the largest I've seen), depending on the club's system and what machine you are playing. When you actually earn a point, the reader flashes "Congratulations [Your Name]," and then something like "Your current session points are 1." Again, not all systems tell you the countdown or any other point information.

Aside from the type of prizes slot clubs dole out (cash or comps), the most important distinction is the method used to calculate player rewards. A club can reward its players based on how many coins they play (coin-in), how much they win (coin-out), how long they play (time), or how many coins they started out with (buy-in).

Coin-In

This is the simplest method to understand and thankfully the most common. Based on a formula, usually made public, the casino awards points according to how much money is played through the machine. For example, The Mirage gives you a point for every $15 dollars played, Sam's Town adds one point for $1, and the MGM awards ten points per $1. Of course, until we know what the points are worth (i.e., how many are needed to obtain a buffet comp for two or a $1 cash rebate), we cannot accurately evaluate how generous a casino is to its slot club members. Again, I cover that in Chapter 6.

At most coin-in slot clubs, you can check your point total by inserting your card into any machine's reader. After the welcome player bit, most systems will give you your total points and indicate the countdown.

Note that many casinos have a higher countdown for video poker than for slots and give fewer points for quarter play than for dollars. If the countdown is 15 for dollars (meaning you must play $15 to earn a point) and 80 for quarters (which equals $20 for a point), you might only want to play dollars at that casino, if you play there at all. (Don't despair. The Four Queens, Jerry's Nugget, and many Laughlin casinos give more points for quarter than for dollar play.)

A variation on the above scheme is to set every machine in the casino at the same countdown, but to vary the number of points awarded. For example, at the Frontier the countdown for all video poker machines is 30. When you complete the countdown on quarter machines you are awarded 1 point, on dollar machines you get 4 points, and $5 machines give you 20 points.

Coin-Out

At least four casinos (Gold Coast, Barbary Coast, Sands, and Tom's Sunset) award points based on the coins you win or take out, not what you put in. In other words, if you play $400 and win $550, you gain more points from a coin-out than a coin-in system. Conversely, if you play $400 and win $300, you earn fewer points.

Which system is better for the player? Except for rare instances, you will always deposit more money into a machine over the long run than you will remove from it. In other words, if the coin-out casino is advertising a 98% payback, you will get 2% fewer points via a coin-out system than a coin-in.

When playing a coin-out system, it's important to remember not to remove your card until the credit meter is at zero (either by cashing out or tapping out). Since you're credited points for *coin-out*, you have to take out all your coins to accrue all your points.

Buy-In

The Sahara and Santa Fe still use a buy-in system. Every time you purchase change or insert money into the currency slot, you have to call over a casino employee to note your buy-in on a special punch card. These systems can be very profitable to players who remember not to replay the same money over and over. Every so often, cash out, take your coins to the cashier, and trade them in for currency. Take a quick break or go to a change booth or change person and turn your cash back into coin—having the employee punch up the transaction. As long as you're giving them some play, this is quite ethical and acceptable to the casino.

Buying coins that you have no intention of playing and hiding in the casino while you unwrap them, or sneaking them unwrapped out of the casino, is neither ethical nor acceptable and could get you ejected, if not permanently barred. (Some crossroader types will go a step further and generously tip the change person to "accidentally" over-credit their accounts.) Because of these abuses, buy-in systems are an endangered species.

Time

Back in the good old days, slot players wishing to be rated and comped were timed by a change person. Slow play and generous

---

WHY PEOPLE DON'T...

When I see people dropping large amounts of money into slot machines without a slot card in the reader, I frequently ask them why they don't belong to the casino's slot club. Most of the answers (other than "What business is it of yours?") fall into one of six categories. I've listed all six below, followed by a comment or opinion.

What's a slot club?

Even some frequent Las Vegas visitors have never heard of slot clubs. Many assume that the reader accepts an ATM or credit card, whereby losses are charged to your Visa or even your bank account. Many more assume that there is a charge for joining.

I've heard of them, but I don't understand them.

The fault here probably lies more with the casinos than the customer. The resorts spend millions on the systems, personnel, and advertising, but don't properly explain the details to John Q. Public. An effective in-casino marketing effort is often lacking.

I don't gamble enough.

Correction: They don't *think* they gamble enough. Most players (especially locals) would be surprised by how much they gamble. Remember, it's not the twenty-dollar bill you're willing to lose that gets counted, it's how many times that twenty gets run through the machine. A couple, each playing quarter video poker machines for only two hours a month, puts $36,000 a year through the machines, which easily qualifies them for several free meals. I sometimes suspect that many people don't want to know or admit how much they gamble.

Didn't you know that the machine pays less when a slot club card is in it?

Slot players can be an especially superstitious bunch: The machines on the aisles pay better... The machines don't pay as well tipping could boost a player's slot club haul significantly. Today, time comes into play with the slot clubs that employ the "don't ask, won't tell" secretive systems. These clubs claim that comps are based on time; in other words, the amount of time you sit at a machine dictates the reward level. In my experience, this is not the case. As an experiment, I once had two players play one hour each on the same

...JOIN SLOT CLUBS

on three-day weekends... Machines that are paying out big are hot... Machines that have just paid out a jackpot should be avoided...

I won't get into a discussion on slot machine technology here, but I will say that any casino implementing a scheme whereby a slot machine pays less when you insert a slot card would find its executives sweating under a spotlight in the Nevada Gaming Control Board's interrogation room. That is an absolute fact, though I'd bet my lucky rabbit's foot that some slot players will never believe me.

Didn't you know that slot cards are an IRS scheme to get information about winners?

I would laugh out loud at this, except I understand that many people are very touchy about federal-government intrusion in their lives. Most of the folks concerned about taxes don't win at all, while the rest don't win enough for the IRS to care. According to my sources, the IRS has never ordered a Las Vegas-wide search of slot club records so they could catch a particular gambler. Conversely, if you find it necessary to document gambling losses (to offset a big jackpot), the slot club will issue a year-end statement documenting losses at the slots.

I don't want to be on mailing lists.

I belong to more than 75 slot clubs (including those in Reno, Tahoe, and Atlantic City), subscribe to 30 magazines, and buy everything mail order. My postman has a hernia, yet I still look forward to opening the slot club mail! In any given week, I get invited to dine (either free or half-price) at several different restaurants, am offered free tickets to shows, and may even get an invite for a getaway weekend. That sure beats reading the monthly bills, the whatever-a-month club mail, and a letter from my mother telling me that I don't write to her enough!

$1 video poker machine in a casino with a timed slot club. Member A played about 300 hands, member B played approximately 600 hands. When they went up to the slot club booth (and talked to the same person), member B was qualified for twice as many comps as member A. This experiment was repeated in three other "don't ask, won't tell" casinos with the same result, thus indicating that in today's slot club world, a timed system is the equivalent of a coin-in system, except that the casinos supply much less information to the members.

ADDITIONAL CONSIDERATIONS

Countdown Retention

At most casinos, once you stop playing a machine and remove your card, the countdown resets to the maximum requirement. Say the starting countdown is 20 quarters. You play only 19, then pull your card out to leave or switch machines. You'll have to begin anew, with the countdown at 20, the next time you put your card into a machine, even if it's the same machine. My point? Make sure you've earned *your* point before pulling your card.

Other clubs retain the countdown: if you pull your card with one quarter to go, the next time you put a quarter into a machine, it will award you the point. So you can feel free to bounce from machine to machine.

The best way to determine whether the computer resets or retains the countdown is to insert your card, play one coin, and check the number. Then remove your card, re-insert it into the same machine, and recheck the number. If it resets to the starting countdown, you'll know not to remove your card till you've earned the point.

In rare instances (Golden Nugget, Stardust, and Frontier), the countdown is retained by the machine and not the player's card. If someone leaves a machine with the countdown at five, the next player only has to deposit five coins to get the point. In these casinos, find the machine with the lowest countdown before beginning play.

Bonus Times

Many low (or no) cash-rebate slot clubs offer double and triple bonus times. Boomtown frequently has double time during the dead of graveyard shift. The Barbary Coast runs bonus times for an entire month. The best way to find out about these promos is to read your casino mail carefully, especially the slot club newsletters, and scan the ads in the *Las Vegas Review-Journal* or the *Las Vegas Sun*.

In Laughlin, not only are bonus times offered on a regular basis in almost all casinos, but many offer triple and quadruple times for the higher denominations.

Table Play

Some casinos with non-cash-rebate slot clubs (Fiesta, Hard Rock, Rio, Texas) have gathered all the casino action—slots, table games, the sports book, even keno and bingo—under the same award roof. By so doing, these casinos have dovetailed the slot club with the table-game complimentaries system, making it easier for slot club members to become rated table-game players and vice versa.

Rewards for table play are almost always figured (under the subjective appraisal of the floor personnel) by the standard comp equation: average bet times hours played times house advantage times equivalency percentage. In other words, if your average bet is $25 and you play blackjack for an hour (60 hands), the casino figures that you supply it with $1,500 worth of action. The $1,500 is multiplied by the house advantage (usually 2%), then that number ($30) is multiplied by the equivalency ratio (usually 30%-40%), which is the percentage of your expected loss that the casino is prepared to return to you in comps (in this case, you'd get back around $10).

Even if the casino doesn't use slot club accounts for table play, always show your club card whenever you sit down at a table. At the very least, it will prompt the floorperson to fill out a rating slip, so you'll be earning comps while you play. (And again, read *Comp City* by Max Rubin to learn how to work the table game system and maximize comps.)

Point Expiration

Casinos don't want to waste computer space on you if you aren't coming back anytime soon. Most will erase your points (but still save your name and address—Mama didn't raise no fools!) after one year if you don't keep your account active. This is not a concern for a frequent visitor or local resident, but if you're not planning to visit this casino in the next year or so, then use up your points any way you can.

Sign-up Prizes

Many clubs give you a small prize just for signing up. A free margarita at the Fiesta, a $5 food coupon at the MGM, dice at the Stardust, and keychains from everywhere are just a few of the reasons for signing up at as many slot clubs as possible.

User-Friendly

As I stated earlier (and will state again and again), some casinos are upfront about how to earn points and what they're worth, and you can check your totals and countdown at every machine in the joint. Others, such as those using secretive systems, tell you absolutely nothing, as if the entire process is a Department of Defense secret: their booths tend to be backed up with a beg line of members checking and rechecking their point totals and asking, "How much longer do I have to play to get a free buffet?" Thankfully, due to player response, user-friendly seems to be winning the war (though not every battle). Case in point: The Gold Coast's slot club does not pay cash and is not all that generous with prizes and comps (less than .2%), yet the locals vote it the Best Slot Club in Las Vegas year after year. Why? One reason might be that any ten-year-old can figure his parents' points and prizes without assistance.

PICKING THE WINNERS

It's the end of the day. You've joined four different slot clubs and collected three keys chains, two drink coupons (happily redeemed), and a cheap hat you hope your son likes a lot better than you do. Plop down on the bed, pull out your slot club brochures, and review your notes. It's time to sort the clubs into your A, B, and C lists, determining which (if any) of these fine (or otherwise) establishments will get your continued business and how and when you should play.

The Cash Explosion Club at the TNT Casino awards one point for every $1 played on all machines at all levels. Once you stop playing a machine and remove your card, the countdown resets to the maximum requirement. Due to the hotel's consistent four-star reputation, room reservations can be hard to come by, even in the summer.

The Penguin Club at the Antarctica Casino awards one point for every $15 won on dollar machines only. The countdown is retained when you change machines, even if you return a month later. Extra ice cubes are available on request.

The Lookout Club at the brand new Titanic Casino awards a point for every $3 played on dollar and quarter slot machines, and $5 played on nickel machines. Video poker players must run $5 worth of action through quarter and dollar machines to earn the same point, and no points are awarded for nickel video poker play. On Mondays and Tuesdays, players receive double points. The countdown is not retained. The elegant Astor Club gourmet room and the

Lifejacket Buffet consistently win top honors in the annual *Las Vegas Review-Journal* "Best of Las Vegas" poll.

At the Winners Club in the Alamo Casino, the card reader says "Card Accepted" and nothing else. When you asked the slot club booth personnel (the ones sporting the "We Love Slot Players" buttons) about how to earn a free buffet, you were curtly told to "play a while longer."

A quick analysis will allow you to devise an effective playing strategy for all four.

Forget the Alamo.

Relegate Antarctica to the C list if you play only quarters and nickels.

What you do with the TNT and Titanic clubs depends on your needs. An out-of-towner, especially one who frequently comes to Las Vegas on short notice, might put the TNT on his A list in order to guarantee A-list treatment from them, while a local resident with a good appetite would try his luck on the Titanic. Whatever route you go, remember to learn the slot club's fine points to maximize benefits. At either one, avoid removing your card if you are more than 50% of the way to earning your next point. If convenient, play at the Titanic only during double time.

The above analysis is vastly simplified and cannot be completed until we study the benefits of each club.

5

Choosing Your Game—
Slots vs. Video Poker

After you sign up for a slot club but before you begin enjoying major benefits, there's a small intermediate step. It's called gambling. Remember? The reason you came to the casino in the first place?

When you walk onto the casino floor, you'll have two decisions to make: what monetary level to play at (nickels, quarters, dollars, etc.), and what type of machine to play (slots or video poker).

NICKELS, QUARTERS, DOLLARS,
OR FIVE DOLLARS?

The decision to play nickel, quarter, dollar, or five dollar (aka big nickel) machines is primarily based on how much money you have to gamble with. The quick-and-dirty money-management rule for machines is to have 400 betting units per one- to two-hour playing session (if you're playing quarters, for example, bring $100). You'll need 1,600 units for an entire weekend (if you're playing big nickels, bring $8,000). Based on personal experience and a few computer simulations I've run, I tend to agree with these estimates.

Most experts also suggest that you play the maximum coin-in for whatever machine you choose, usually two or three units for slots and five for video poker. This is because the jackpots for maximum coin-in usually pay a bonus relative to the payouts for lesser coin-in. On most video poker machines, you win 250 coins for a royal flush with one coin played. From there, the royal payout rises by 250 coins per additional coin played: 500 for 2 coins, 750 for 3, and 1,000 for 4. But the payout for the maximum 5 coins is 4,000 coins (instead of 1,250), a hefty bonus.

Video poker expert Bob Dancer suggests that risk-averse players consider playing only one coin per game. This strategy assures that you will part with less money over time, especially if you are playing a machine with a large house advantage (and that includes all slot machines). For some, the great fear in making this move is that they'll hit a jackpot, especially a royal flush, with fewer than maximum coins played. True, it hurts, but the chances of hitting a royal are about 1 in 40,000 hands (or once every 80 hours), so the odds are slim that you'll actually feel the pain. But if you play "short-coin," understand that you will accumulate a lot fewer slot points and benefits.

There are clear-cut advantages to playing one quarter instead of five nickels. In many instances, a quarter machine played with one coin pays a higher percentage than a nickel machine with maximum coins, and if the casino doesn't pay slot club benefits for nickel play, then it's a slam dunk that you should play one quarter.

The advantages in moving up from five quarters to a single dollar (or more accurately, moving down from $1.25 to $1) in video poker are less definite. Due to the loss of the bonus for short-coin dollar play, this move will raise your expected loss per play. The only time you should consider it is when the slot club does not count quarters. Even then, you'll need to get some value beyond a cash rebate (comps or discounts) in order to make up the difference.

SLOT MACHINES

Slot machines and the people who play them get a bad rap, particularly from video poker players. What video poker players seem to overlook is that slot players have a very different set of goals. Many video poker players are actively trying to beat the house and a few are even looking for a long-term source of income. I have never met a slot player, on the other hand, who believed that he or she could make a living playing the slots.

Slot players are out to have fun in the casino. Of course, the possibility of hitting a big jackpot is always on their minds, but even if they don't hit the big one, they still have a good time. The majority of slot players are tourists who visit Las Vegas a couple of times a year and have neither the time, nor the inclination, to learn elaborate video poker strategies.

In Las Vegas, quarter and dollar slots have an average payback of 93%-97%. On top of that, add .5%-1% for a slot club's cash rebate and you have up to a 98% return. Sure you can do better at video poker, but a 94%-98% slot return requires no study, no practice, and no analysis, and it certainly beats the return at the other no-training-required games, such as roulette, big 6, or keno.

When choosing a slot machine, remember that during losing sessions you will lose your money faster playing machines with extremely high jackpots. The casino has to win more money from most of the players to be able to pay the lucky few who win the jackpots. In the gambling biz, this loss when you don't hit the big prize is known as the "drain." Since it's extremely unlikely that you'll hit the big jackpot if you play Quartermania or Megabucks, you'll have to be prepared to endure the sizable drain that goes with playing those machines. If that's your preferred excitement, well, it's your money. Machines with top jackpots of less than 5,000 coins have a much lower drain, so you'll get many more interim payoffs, which will allow you to play longer and pile up more slot club points.

Where are the best slot machines located? According to Nevada Gaming Control Board statistics, the best machines can be found downtown and at the outlier casinos located on Boulder Highway and Rancho Drive. Think twice before playing a machine outside of a casino, such as those at car washes, supermarkets, convenience stores, or even glorified bars that call themselves casinos. These places don't have a sufficient volume of players to offer good paybacks, they don't have slot clubs, and if you do get lucky and hit a jackpot, you might have to wait an hour or more to collect (the machines are maintained by route operators, and it usually takes awhile for the drivers to get there). A good rule of thumb is: if table games aren't available, the slot machines are probably a bad bet.

In the final section of this book I assign separate ratings to each casino's selection of video poker machines. Though there is no documented evidence to back this up (Nevada does not subdivide its revenue-reporting figures by individual casinos), it's reasonable to assume that a casino with excellent video poker will also have good slot machines.

VIDEO BLACKJACK

Video blackjack has been on the casino floor for years, and has never gotten much attention. Why not? Most blackjack machines pay even money on naturals (blackjack), as opposed to the 3-2 paid at the tables. Though it may not seem like a big deal, that little adjustment costs the player about 2.3% in expected return, so anyone who knows the game ignores the machines. Anyone who doesn't know the game also ignores the machines.

On the other hand, slot players should consider video blackjack. A basic strategy blackjack player can play these machines with about a 97.5% return, which is higher than most slot machines. Even players who don't know basic strategy can attain about a 96% return, which is still not bad, especially if the slot club rebate is 1% or better.

VIDEO KENO

Beware! At the nickel level, video keno returns only about 85%, possibly more with a high progressive meter. At the quarter level, the casino usually pays back about 92%, less than most quarter slots.

Though these paybacks are a considerable improvement over live keno (which runs in the 70% return range), video keno moves about a hundred times faster. The large drain created by the top-heavy jackpots, combined with the speed of the game, will wipe out the average player's bankroll in no time.

The one advantage to video keno is that a skilled player can analyze the payoff schedules and determine which casino offers the best machines. If you live for video keno, buy a book on the game and learn to pick the best of the bunch. If you find a good quarter progressive game (possibly 94% or better) combined with a good slot club, go for it.

VIDEO POKER

Video poker's popularity exploded in the mid-1980s, and the machines grabbed coveted casino space from both slot machines and table games. Anthony Curtis, publisher of the *Las Vegas Advisor*, has written that video poker's popularity is due to a powerful combination of features. It's derived from the popular game of poker. It's unintimidating. There's the possibility of a big payoff. It's fast. Players have control and believe they can win. And the investment to play can be low.

Video poker is very popular with Las Vegas locals, especially women. Almost every Las Vegas lounge has video poker machines built into the bars, with plenty of additional machines strategically placed throughout the joints.

Unlike slots, video poker can be played for profit. Some schedules return in excess of 100% for perfect play, and the player's advantage is compounded when slot club benefits are added. Even schedules with a slightly negative return, such as jacks or better, can be made into a profitable game if the slot club cash rebate is high enough. In addition to a steady income, professional players can get free rooms, meals, and T-shirts bearing the name of their current employer.

Pros aren't the only winners. Any casual player who takes the time to learn proper video poker strategy and joins a few slot clubs can reduce, and sometimes eliminate, the primary expenses of a Las Vegas vacation.

Unfortunately, the reality is that most video poker players play so poorly that they would actually do better playing the slot machines. While it's true that expert machine selection and perfect play will yield a 100% return (or better), poor selection and bad play can drop the return into the low 90s. This is neither the time nor the place to teach the fine (and profitable) art of playing video poker, but I'll try to provide enough information to allow you to organize a battle plan. At the end of this chapter are sources for further study.

The first important decision a video poker player makes is choosing which machine to play. There are dozens of variations, but they generally fall into three categories: jacks or better, bonus poker, and wild cards.

Jacks Or Better

The original and still the easiest to learn. All jacks machines return your bet for a pair of jacks, queens, kings, or aces (hence the name). They all return 2 units for two pair, 3 for three-of-a-kind, 4 for a straight, 25 for four-of-a-kind, and 50 for a straight flush. Jacks or better machines differ in the payouts for a flush, a full house, and a royal flush. Generally, the best pay schedule you can expect to find (on a non-progressive machine) returns 9 units for a full house, 6 for a flush, and 4,700 coins for a royal flush with a full five-coin bet (our shorthand is 9/6-4700 jacks). This schedule has a long-term expected return for perfect play of 99.9%. In other words, for every $1,000 you play in this machine, you expect to get back $999. Combine this return with any form of slot club and you have an edge over the casino.

The next best case, and the standard for jacks, is a machine that returns 9 units for a full house, 6 for a flush, and has a 5-coin jackpot of 4,000 coins (aka 9/6 jacks). With perfect play, you can achieve a return of 99.5%. Farther down the payout pecking order are the 8/5 jacks, returning only 8 units for a full house and 5 for a flush (97.3% with a 4,000-coin royal). The 8/5 machines often come with progressive royal flushes. Serious video poker players ignore these machines unless the progressive jackpot is at least 8,800 coins ($440 for nickels, $2,200 for quarters, $8,800 for dollars, and $44,000 for five dollars) for a 5-coin royal flush.

Bonus Poker

This game is basic 8/5 jacks that pays bonuses for various four-of-a-kinds. The most common bonus poker machine returns 80 units for four aces, 40 for four 2s, 3s, or 4s, and the standard 25 for four 5s through four kings. The return percentage is 99.2%. Another version called aces & faces pays 40 units for four kings, queens, and jacks (as opposed to the 2s, 3s, and 4s) and returns 99.3%. Both require only a slightly different strategy than 9/6 jacks. (Note: Bonus poker also comes in 7/5 and 6/5. These should be avoided.)

Recently, double bonus poker has caught on. It pays 160 units for four aces, 80 for four 2s, 3s or 4s, and 50 for all other four-of-a-kinds. But it only pays even money for two pair. Though the 10/7 version of double bonus poker (10 units for a full house, 7 for a flush) can yield the expert a 100.2% return, don't go near this game unless you've really mastered its fine points. Bob Dancer is an expert and plays double bonus machines all the time. I'm not, so I don't.

Wild Cards

A few years ago, joker poker was a popular game. Today, there are so few of these machines (with decent returns) left in Las Vegas that I won't even discuss them. On the other hand, there are still plenty of profitable deuces wild machines. The full-pay version pays 800 for a royal flush, 200 for four deuces, 25 for a wild royal flush, 15 for five-of-a-kind, 9 for a straight flush, 5 for four-of-a-kind, 3 for a full house, 2 for a flush or straight, and 1 for three-of-a-kind, and has a return for perfect play of 100.7%. Again, this is a game that requires extensive training and expert play to achieve the positive return. (For a complete rundown of video poker payoff schedules, see Chapter 8.)

Earning And Learning

Keep in mind that the above percentages include the return for hitting the royal flush. Hitting a royal is an infrequent event (approximately 1 in 40,000 hands) so it could take a long time for these percentages to be realized. How long is long? That depends on the game, your strategy, and the gods. I've run several million-hand simulations on my computer, in which the number of hands played before a royal flush showed up varied greatly, even with perfect play.

So how do you learn to play video poker? First, buy a book on the subject. For the absolute beginner who needs to start from ground zero, *Bargain City* by Anthony Curtis provides the most basic video poker training. For more advanced treatment, the three standard video poker books are Lenny Frome's *Winning Strategies for Video Poker*, Dan Paymar's *Video Poker—Precision Play*, and Stanford Wong's *Professional Video Poker*. All are good, none are great. My fellow writer Bob Dancer has a book in the works tentatively titled *Video Poker for Winners* and I look toward to its publication day with great anticipation.

A VIDEO POKER PRO'S TOP TEN

A new breed of professional gambler, the video poker pro, combines perfect play with slot club returns to achieve a steady (albeit erratic) income of $10-$50 an hour. While the usual choice of weapon is a full-pay deuces or double bonus machine (both games have a theoretical return greater than 100%), a pro will occasionally drop down to 9/6 jacks or better or even 8/5 jacks progressives, as long as either the slot club rebate or the progressive jackpot makes the move worthwhile.

The lifestyle of these gamblers is less than enviable. Forget Simon Templar and Doc Holliday. Most video poker pros (primarily Las Vegas locals) spend 4-8 hours a day sitting alone in a casino, (usually at 4 a.m.), staring at five cards on a video screen.

You may be inconvenienced by a video poker pro (or even a team of pros) attacking a positive-expectation situation, so in order to understand what's happening at the machines, from the home office in northwest Las Vegas, here are the top ten ways to spot video poker pros:

10. They remove their slot card when they're dealt a winning hand. (Pros are afraid that the casino won't buy them dinner if they know how much they win.)
9. If they hit a royal flush and there's still ten minutes left before midnight on double-point day, they move to the next machine and keep playing.
8. When you hit a royal flush and start screaming, they tell you to stop making a scene over something so common.
7. When asked to list their next of kin on a legal form, they write down their slot host.
6. They know the words to every song that's played over the casino's PA system.
5. They have all the attributes that Bill Gates has, except the 14 billion dollars.
4. If you win a $2,000 jackpot on a quarter 8/5 jacks progressive, they tell you how stupid you are for playing a machine with less than a 100% theoretical return.
3. They know what "SF 3di 0hi (with no straight interference) - 9hi higher than QT" actually means. Worse yet, they care.
2. They will ask, in complete sincerity, "O.J. who?"
1. They never seem to be having any fun.

If you have a personal computer, buy a video poker software program. Either *Stanford Wong Video Poker* or the much harder-to-find *Video Poker Tutor* by Panamint will do the job. If you don't have a computer, I strongly suggest you get one.

Video poker strategy cards can be found in gambling bookstores and gift shops. Similar in size and shape to slot club cards, strategy cards can be used in the casino when you cannot remember how to play a particular hand. Even expert players use them, and I have never heard of a casino confiscating a strategy card or telling a video poker player to put one away. The best cards are homemade, based on strategies you have either researched in books or developed on a computer.

RISKY BUSINESS

Here's the warning on your medicine bottle.

Never (as in forever) gamble solely to obtain a comp. Never increase your bet level to obtain additional slot club benefits. And never play with money needed for another purpose. If you gamble away more money than you can afford, whether $50 or $5,000, no free meal in the world will relieve that sinking feeling in the pit of your stomach.

It's important to realize that the payback percentages quoted in this book are averages that include the return for hitting a machine's top jackpot. Since you probably won't hit four Megabucks symbols or even a video poker royal flush during a session, many of your playing sessions will result in losses, and often at a rate that exceeds the expected loss. It's possible to lose as much as $150 in a bad one-hour session of quarter slots or video poker (that's $600 for dollars and $3,000 for five dollars).

The Benefits

Now for the fun! You've played for a few hours (or days) and it's time to collect your hard-earned reward(s)—cash, dinner for two, or a sweatshirt to die for. First, check your watch. Though the situation is changing, few slot club booths are open 24 hours a day. Many close by midnight or 2 a.m. and do not reopen until 9 the following morning. Even if the booth is open, before you run back to claim what's yours, let's regroup for another strategy session. Remember, the more you know, the farther you'll go. Anyone can cash in points and get whatever the club says they're worth, but knowledgeable slot club members get a great deal more.

Slot club benefits can be divided into two categories: tangible and intangible. Tangible benefits, whether cash, comps, or merchandise, are directly related to your point balance and are issued on a completely objective basis determined by the computer. They are usually spelled out in the club's written material and any employee in the booth can give them to you. Intangible benefits have to be discovered, and to the best combination of detective, diplomat, and behavioral researcher goes the spoils. (Just visualize the team of Holmes, Kissinger, and Pavlov at a slot machine and you will get the idea.)

TANGIBLE BENEFITS

Getting the most out of the tangible benefits requires information and some entry-level mathematical analysis (i.e., a little arithmetic). Not only do you have to compare casino to casino, you must be able to compare the value of one benefit to another. (Should I redeem my points for cash, a comp, or a prize?)

Cash

Though more than 50% of slot clubs award cash rebates, there are major differences in the bottom-line amounts. For example, for

$100 coin-in, the Cal Club at the California rebates 10¢, the Golden Nugget's 24 Karat Club rebates 67¢, and the Celebrity Club at the Desert Inn gives back $1. All for the same $100 in action.

On the surface, it seems that if you want the highest cash rebate your choice is obvious: just compare the percentages and choose the DI. Unfortunately, it's not that simple. Slot clubs seldom publish their cash-rebate percentages, which means you have to compute the figures on your own. You'll need to know two things: the countdown, which is the number of plays required to earn a point, and the number of points needed to earn a $1 cash rebate. We discussed how to check the countdown in Chapter Four. Finding out how many points earn $1 is usually easier, as most casinos will tell you straight up in their literature or if you ask at the booth. To get the cash-rebate percentage, divide $1 by the product of the countdown and the number of points required to earn $1. The equation is: $1 \div (cp)$, where c = countdown and p = points required to earn $1.

Here's an example. At the Golden Nugget you have to run $75 through a $1 slot or video poker machine to earn one point (c = 75). You get a $1 cash rebate for every 2 points (p = 2). The cash rebate percentage equation looks like this: $1 \div (75 \times 2) = .0067$ or .67%. Which means that for every $100 played at the Golden Nugget, you're returned 67¢, assuming you use your slot club card. Thus, members of the 24 Karat Club who play a $1 video poker machine 500 times an hour for two hours are $33.50 richer than non-members ($5 per play x 500 hands x 2 hours x .0067 rebate percentage).

Another example: The Four Queens requires that 32 coins be played through a quarter video poker machine ($8) to earn a point, and rebates $1 for every 40 points. What is the cash rebate return percentage? Answer: $1 \div (8 \times 40) = .31\%$

Let's take a look at what this means. If your game of choice is jacks or better and you're playing a 9/6 machine, your expected return without the slot club is 99.5%. If you add a cash-back return percentage of .67%, you raise the expected return to 100.17%. Now you're *making* money, figuring to earn 17¢ on every $100 you put into action ($99.50 + 67¢ = $100.17). Please remember that perfect play, a large bankroll, and a great deal of time are necessary to make this possible.

When you analyze cash-back returns, take particular note of the dates for double- or triple-point sessions (if the club has them). During bonus periods, a .25% return can suddenly become a .50% or .75% return.

Some sort of minimum point total is required to get your first cash rebate (usually the amount necessary to get back $10). Be sure to go to the booth and redeem your points as soon as you make this

requirement or by the end of your trip at the latest. There is no
advantage to carrying cash-rebate points over long periods of time.
You might forget that you have them and never get the money at
all, or the points could expire if you don't return to Las Vegas within
one year. (The MGM Grand is an exception. The more points you
have, the higher percentage of cash you receive. If you expect to
return within the year, hold on to your points.)

After checking your photo ID, the club issues a payment voucher
that resembles a check. It is not a check. Payment vouchers can
only be redeemed at the casino cashier and there's often a stipula-
tion that redemption be within 24 hours from time of issue. Treat it
as you would any other paycheck and take it directly to the cage.
Ask for good old American greenbacks and walk them out the door.
Do not use the voucher in the gift shop or restaurants unless you
plan to spend the entire amount, because they will not give you
change.

Comps/Scrip

Though the situation is changing, free rooms and meals (no cash
back) are still the only slot club awards at a surprising number of
casinos.

Before you do anything else, determine what is being offered, a
comp or scrip. A comped meal allows you to go into the casino coffee
shop and eat like a sailor on shore leave. Help yourself to an appe-
tizer, an a la carte salad, the most expensive entree, a dessert, and
beverages. By yourself, you can run up a $25 tab with very little
work. Don't be shy, you've earned it, and it'll only cost you the tip.

Scrip, on the other hand, limits your splurge to a certain dollar
amount, maybe enough to cover the meat loaf special and coffee
(and you're still responsible for the tip).

A room comp usually includes everything (except long-distance
telephone calls and in-room movies). Scrip applied to a room charge
only covers a certain dollar amount, leaving you to fund any unpaid
difference in the bill, along with the room tax (8% on the Strip, 9%
downtown), telephone charges, and other incidentals.

If comps or scrip are the only tangible benefit offered by the
club, you should again figure a return percentage. At the Barbary
Coast, dinner for two in the coffee shop requires 12,500 points. You
need to play about $12,500 to earn 12,500 points (more or less, since
the Barbary has a coin-out system). To equal a decent .4% return,
you will have to consume $50 worth of coffee shop food (50 ÷ 12,500
= .004). Bring a hungry friend!

If the club offers a choice of comps or cash, take the comp only
if you really want it and its value is greater than the cash it re-

places. At the majority of slot clubs the comp is indeed worth more. For example, at the Riviera, 200 points will get you either $10 cash, $11 scrip for the coffee shop, or two buffets valued at $14. (An important exception is the Las Vegas Hilton, where scrip is worth less than cash, on the theory that scrip walks out of the casino to be redeemed in the restaurants or gift shops, while a cash rebate will probably go right back into the slot machines.)

Before accepting a food comp, double-check what restaurant and which meal the comp is for, when the comp expires, and if it includes use of the VIP line. You will be asked to show photo ID when the comp is issued at the booth, but not when you show up at the restaurant, so it's not unusual for comps to wind up in a secondary market, being sold, bartered, or given away as gifts.

A final point on comps. It may be possible to obtain your desired room or free meal without using up club points, so invest your points only after you've exhausted all the other routes to the comp.

Prizes/Merchandise

Slot clubs frequently give out items such as a T-shirt or cheap piece of luggage imprinted with the casino logo just for reaching a certain play level, with no points deducted. If that is not the case, I consider it foolish to use up your points to be someone else's walking billboard, unless the T-shirt is a really good deal. At Circus Circus casinos, the value of the various T-shirts is considerably higher than the equivalent cash rebate, but at many other places, it is usually cheaper and far easier to buy the item in the gift shop.

The Gold Coast offers a complete redemption catalog full of toaster ovens, VCRs, even a Hawaiian vacation. Calculating the return percentage by assigning a representative value to the merchandise, the Gold Coast's average return is less than .2%. A member would do better buying the item at Wal-Mart and using the Gold Coast points at one of the casino's good restaurants.

If you are redeeming points for prizes, the slot club staff will honor the redemption schedule to the letter, except if they are out of stock on the item you select. Then you might be offered an upgrade to a more valuable prize at no additional cost, especially if you act a tad disappointed.

INTANGIBLE BENEFITS

Now for the advanced class!

I define "intangible" as any benefit you receive from the slot club that does not affect (or reduce) your point total. This can be a free room or meal, a free tournament, a shopping discount, or some other form of special VIP treatment. Though intangible benefits are determined by the amount and level of your play, you receive them along with (not instead of) your tangible benefits. Sort of like having your cake and your cash, too.

For example, Sam's Town will usually treat you to a dinner for two at Papamio's, its upscale Italian restaurant, after you play $2,500 in a slot or video poker machine. Slightly more play at the Golden Nugget will get you a champagne brunch for two. Next door at the Four Queens, $3,000 in action gets you two meals at Magnolia's coffee shop.

All these intangible benefits are doled out in addition to your cash rebate, thus raising the overall slot club return. The moral of the story is that the stated benefits offered by the slot club are really the minimum benefits available.

The bad news is that the casino seldom volunteers information about intangible benefits. Management is wary of video poker professionals who augment their livelihoods with comps, as well as savvy bargain hunters who reap the benefits but only gamble the absolute minimum necessary to get them. And unlike tangible benefits, which are so publicized that they are practically carved in stone, an intangible benefit policy can be changed via a

MAINTAINING YOUR MEMBERSHIPS

Slot clubs wipe out unredeemed points after a year or eighteen months. After three years, the computer may eliminate your entire record. The simple way to find out if your points are still in a club's system after your account has been inactive for a year or more is to go to the booth (or call) and ask. If your points are intact, a short play serves to extend your active status. A common worry is that this minimum play will negatively impact your status, i.e., label you as a little player. If this is an A-list club where you've played big in the past, you'll always be able to bring that to the attention of whomever might be questioning your status. If it's not A-list, then it doesn't really matter.

Locals and frequent visitors should pay special attention to A and B clubs. Slot club policies change constantly. You should know how much play is required to maintain your favorite privileges.

Once-per-year visitors should restrict their play to their favorite places, and make sure to redeem all points before going home after each trip.

Monday morning memo.

To get the most from intangibles, you should read all the club's written material carefully, especially the newsletter, make an effort to pick up tidbits from other members, be friendly and courteous toward the staff and other customers, and most importantly, develop a good relationship with a slot host.

In my experience, slot hosts are much more generous with comps than club booth personnel. Slot hosts are hired to keep good players happy, whereas booth personnel are rewarded for keeping their noses clean. Also, a slot host can write a comp without having to clear it with anyone else, while slot booth personnel usually have to track down a superior (such as a slot host!) for permission. If the people at the booth are having a hectic day, they'd rather get rid of you quickly (which is accomplished by saying no).

Time for the plunge. After giving the casino about $2,000 in slot play (maybe more for video poker), ask a change person or cashier to send over a slot host. *Do not* go to the slot club booth, but stay seated at the machine, entranced. Hosts are much more generous when dealing with a player in action versus a beggar.

If this is the first time you've met, introduce yourself as a new customer and ask politely about a meal comp. An opening line such as "Can you check to see if I've qualified for a free buffet?" works best. Never demand, and don't lie about how long you've played or how much you've lost, as that information is already in the computer. On your first attempt, be satisfied and gracious about a buffet or coffee shop comp for two. If you are offered more than that, all the better. (Two rules of the road apply here. First, be aware of how important your play is to that particular casino; four hours of quarter slot play will go farther at the San Remo than across the street at the MGM Grand. Second, try to find a host of the opposite sex. It has been my experience that a male player will get better treatment from a female host, and vice versa.)

Once you've popped the comp question, one of three things will happen. One, the host will say yes on the spot. Two, the host will ask for your card, disappear to check the computer, then come back and say yes. Three, the host will say no, either on the spot or after checking the computer, and tell you how much more play you need. Whatever happens, you are no worse off than when you started. You also have a rough idea of what $2,000 (more or less) worth of action gets you at this casino.

If the transaction goes well, ask the host for his card, and find out what days he works. After you've done this a few times, you'll develop a list of hosts and their vital statistics, which you can review before you visit your favorite casino. By keeping track of who the good and bad hosts are, your comp-hustle comfort level will increase. You'll also begin to look and feel like one of the regulars. That's because you are.

If you develop an especially good rapport with a host, it's not bad form to inquire, in a friendly or off-hand way, about the method the casino uses to determine extra meal comps. The host might give you a general idea: perhaps intangibles are based on amount of play that day, amount of play on your last trip, or amount on your last three visits. Obviously, you don't go into this much detail with a host at every joint you walk into, but if this is an A- or B-list casino, every little tidbit of information can pad your edge.

This advice goes double if you're in a casino with a secretive system. Never ever go to the booth and ask for a comp unless you are dealing with a bona fide host (which is unlikely, because hosts generally hate hanging around the booth).

For even better results in the "don't ask, won't tell" joints, try it this way. After you've played for an hour or so at one monetary level, go to the next higher coin denomination, say quarters to dollars. Make sure it's a slot or video keno machine (not video poker). Call for a host and play one coin at a time until he arrives. Make max-coin bets for a few rounds while chatting with the host, then ask for the comp. Because secretive systems tell the players absolutely nothing, the slot hosts have to do a lot more running around answering mundane questions, and are often short on time. The host will usually assume that you're a high-end slot player (their favorite customers), and write you the comp on the spot.

Treat your host well. Thank him personally after each free meal and, every so often, write a note to his boss about how great he is. Bring him other customers. If you should win a big jackpot and your host is around to congratulate you, offer him a nice tip (if he can accept it, he can do a lot more for you than all the change people who suddenly appear when the buzzers go off). Get to know him as a person. Ask about his family, hobbies, or the favorite topic of most hosts, his previous employer. A little effort with the host costs nothing and can really increase your return.

The other major intangible is free or heavily discounted hotel rooms. Depending on when you want the room (mid-December is easy, New Year's Eve is impossible), slot club members who provide $2,000 a day or more in action should automatically receive the casino rate, on average a 50% discount on a room, without any affect on their point totals. If you already belong to the club, make the reservations through its 800 number and the slot club staff will handle the reservation and discount. If you know a host, call him.

For first-time visitors, the drill is different. After you check in, go in person to the booth or contact a host to ask how much play is required to adjust your bill to reflect the casino rate. After you've completed the amount of play that's required, go back to the booth or host and ask to have your rate adjustment put through the system. Make sure you get the name of whomever helps you. Later that day (or early the next), call the front desk to see if the rate change was put through. Frequently, room-rate adjustments for current hotel guests get lost and you don't find this out until checkout time.

Casinos are ten times more generous in giving the casino rate than they are in comping a room, so be aware of the amount of play required to jump from one level to the next. You probably don't want to commit to six hours of slot play just to save a mere $30 on your room rate, especially when that same play could be applied to $80 in free meals. The best time to inquire about free rooms is after you've been granted the casino rate. Just ask the host. By then he knows he has a real player on his hands, and he'll be more interested in accommodating you.

Some slot clubs, especially those at the Frontier, Westward Ho, Four Queens, and Hacienda, are given a block of rooms to distribute to active members; this doesn't affect their overall point totals. The best place to get all the details is in the newsletters or other printed materials you receive in the mail.

OTHER INTANGIBLES

Free rooms and food are the two most important intangibles, but many other side benefits also add to the overall value of your membership.

Direct Mailings And Newsletters

The primary reason I tell you to sign up for all the slot clubs you can is to be on the receiving end of their various direct-mail programs. I recently received a total of seven free-night offers from different casinos in Laughlin. All I did was sign up and play for a half hour in each casino.

At the very least, scan every piece of mail you receive from a casino, even if it's an invitation to a slot tournament you would never attend. Frequently, you'll find two-for-one coupons or other discounts. Casinos with large showrooms, such as Caesars Palace, sometimes send out offers for free tickets to see even the most in-demand headliners. If you're interested, call the casino immediately. Free seats fill up fast.

A SLOT CLUB FOR KIDS?

Not quite, but Treasure Island has the closest thing, the Mutiny Bay Club. It's open to kids of all ages.

Deep inside the resort (at the end of the shopping mall, next to the *Cirque du Soleil* theater) is Mutiny Bay, a first-class arcade featuring carnival games, video machines, and even a simulated auto race using a full-size car. The games run from 25¢ to several dollars. A couple of active children can go through more money in a weekend at Mutiny Bay than their parents might spend elsewhere at Treasure Island.

In the arcade are several "redemption games" (including skee-ball, rock & bowl, cyclone, etc.) that issue winners a predetermined number of tickets. Players can redeem the tickets for prizes, starting at keyrings and whistles and topping off at extravagant items like hair-dryers, toaster ovens, and boom-box radios.

Upon sign-up Mutiny Bay members are given a card (darn!, it doesn't work in the machines outside the arcade) and a special account number. Both members and non-members can play the games, collect, and then immediately redeem tickets, but members have the additional option of depositing their tickets into their account for use at a later time. Thus a frequent visitor can get bigger prizes by combining his winnings from several trips. Members receive quarterly statements and a newsletter containing various specials, including double-ticket coupons.

Tickets can only be redeemed for merchandise, not free meals or rooms. Mutiny Bay Club members are not eligible for the casino rate, either. Let's organize a bunch of Seabees and speak to the captain about that.

Active members receive the club newsletter, which includes a calendar detailing double-point days, free nights, almost-free weekends, etc. The newsletters are the best source of miscellaneous intangible benefits and should be read from cover to cover. Too bad there isn't a quiz at the end!

The best mail arrives the month of your birthday, your spouse's birthday, or your anniversary. Make a list of all items received, detailing which casino sent them, what the gift is, what you have to do to obtain it, and especially, what the expiration date of the offer is. If you don't plan on coming to Las Vegas before the offer expires, call the slot club manager or your casino host as soon as possible and request an extension. Someone in authority will usually accommodate you.

Free Games

This is one of my favorite intangibles. At the Four Queens, slot club members who earn 5,000 lifetime points ($20,000 coin-in on quarter slots, $40,000 for video poker) are invited to a monthly bingo game, absolutely free. You get to play twelve games with jackpots of $50-$300. At the Fremont across the street, club members get a free daily pull on a special slot machine that awards an occasional cash jackpot and, more frequently, tickets that can be accumulated toward prizes. Anyone who earns $8 worth of MVP bucks at Bally's (don't ask me how, they use a secretive system) gets to participate in a daily slot tournament with a top prize of $750. All are good deals for the price—nothing.

Members are always first to be notified about slot and video poker tournaments. These tournaments frequently come with free rooms, drinks, gifts, and even gourmet meals, along with a usual 100% return on all entry fees as prize money. Some of these tournaments are marathons where all points accumulated over a set time period are credited to your regular account, redeemable for cash or comps.

Win/Loss Records

If you hit a jackpot of $1,200 or more on a slot or video poker machine, you must sign an IRS form W-2G before receiving the winnings. Come next April 15, these winnings must be claimed as income on your tax return. If you can't prove any offsetting losses, you'll have to pay tax on the entire amount. Upon request, almost every slot club will send you, at no charge, a year-end statement showing your win-and-loss record at that casino.

Shopping Discounts

More and more casinos are giving their slot club members 10%-20% discounts at company-owned shops located on the premises. Members of the Emperors Club at Caesars Palace automatically (no play required) receive a 10% discount at several of the shops in the Forum next door. Whenever you buy items featuring the casino's logo or name, ask the sales clerk if slot club members get a discount. This benefit is especially valuable when buying souvenirs or gifts.

Over-55 Clubs

Casinos know who butters their bread, and the over-55 set packs a lot of Mazola, especially at the joints hustling the local crowd. At the Santa Fe, senior members of the Players Club can participate in low-entry-fee blackjack and video poker tournaments that include a discounted buffet lunch. Every month, the Four Queens has a special free bingo session for its Club 55 members. Unlike the free bingo mentioned above, Club 55 members need only 500 lifetime points to participate.

Priority Treatment

The universal intangible. When you're a slot club member, you are a VIP. Every request, be it room and dinner reservations, show tickets, late check-out, baby-sitting, even airline assistance, should go through your slot host or the slot club booth. You play at their casino. You've given them your name, address, and most important, your action. You *are* special. If the casino hasn't figured that out, go elsewhere. There are more than fifty slot clubs in southern Nevada and the number is increasing every year.

HOW LONG DOES IT TAKE TO PLAY $2,000?

	FAST		AVERAGE		SLOW	
	Slots	VP	Slots	VP	Slots	VP
5¢	30 hrs	10 hrs	35 hrs	15 hrs	40 hrs	20 hrs
25¢	6 hrs	2 hrs	7 hrs	3 hrs	8 hrs	4 hrs
$1	1 1/2 hrs	1/2 hr	1 3/4 hrs	3/4 hr	2 hrs	1 hr
$5	18 min	6 min	21 min	9 min	25 min	12 min

Use this chart to estimate amount of time required to satisfy slot club play requirements. The figures are based on $2,000 coin-in, which is a common requirement for full-membership activation and consideration for low-level intangibles. If a requirement is greater, simply multiply by the number necessary (if $4,000 is needed, multiply estimated time by 2). Divide if a requirement is less. Remember that these are estimates. Two variables—your playing speed and the number of coins you're playing—will affect your actual results.

The Best Club?

What's the best slot club in Las Vegas? I can't answer that question, until I know who you are. Different people use different slot clubs for different purposes, whether for a cheap holiday, a luxurious vacation, a free meal, a principal source of income, or even a fun way to meet people.

A good slot club is one that enhances the enjoyment at the casino where you're playing. It might even augment your bankroll while you play. But a slot club alone shouldn't be the defining reason in choosing a casino to play in. Several other factors must be considered before that decision can be made.

For most, the first consideration will be the machines. Does the casino have the machines that you want to play? Serious video poker players avoid casinos that do not offer at least 9/6 jacks. For example, The Mirage has a great .67% cash rebate and lousy machines. The Frontier up the street, on the other hand, offers comps only (no cash rebate), but great machines. You will find the veteran in-the-know players at the latter. If you play only quarters or certain types of slots, such as Quartermania or Megabucks, you'll want a casino that includes your favorite slot machines in its mix.

Another consideration is the non-machine action. If you like to play table games, you'll have to do some additional research. Rules and minimums differ from casino to casino, so you'll have to locate a casino where both the slot club and the table games meet your needs. If blackjack is your game, check out Stanford Wong's *Current Blackjack News* (Pi Yee Press, 7910 Ivanhoe #34, La Jolla, California 92037, 619/456-4080; $79 a year) for the latest on rules and promotions in every casino.

You should also appraise the overall ambience of the casino. The MGM Grand and the Nevada Palace have few customers in common. Where are you most comfortable?

How about the restaurants? Meal comps, especially the buffet, are still the most popular and common non-cash benefit a slot club offers. The video poker might be great and the slot club generous, but if the buffet is losing customers to the city mission, then why spend time qualifying for something that you don't want?

Other factors might include location (Strip, downtown, Boulder Highway, Rancho Drive), child care, bowling, the color of the carpet, the cleavage of the waitresses, the attitude of the staff, or even the casino's history of labor relations.

CASE STUDIES

To illustrate the point (and have some fun), I've created the following scenarios based on the true stories of actual players I know.

The Big Player

Jim Lincoln is a high roller. He and his wife Laura (and occasionally their kids) come to Las Vegas at least four times a year. Jim plays $5 (even $25) video poker, while Laura sticks to dollar slots. In any given weekend, their total action exceeds $250,000, which is why Jim is on the A-list of every slot host in town.

The Lincoln's A-list casinos are the MGM, Desert Inn, and Treasure Island. Why? Because their slot clubs have generous cash rebates. At Jim's level of action, any casino he chooses will give him a full comp for his room, food, and beverage, so he's looking for that extra cash bonus—in his case, $2,000 or more per trip. Before coming to Las Vegas, Jim contacts the hosts (if they haven't called him first) and plays one against the others until he gets the best deal. If his children and their friends are in tow, family-style amenities might be the deciding factor (Jim feels that Treasure Island, with its pool, Mutiny Bay arcade, and nightly pirate fight, accommodates children better than any other comparable property). Another factor is that his wife's favorite restaurant is the Buccaneer Bay Club.

Jim's advice: Treat your slot hosts better than you treat your mother, especially when they're fighting over you.

Expert Economizer

Beth Windsor and her husband Phil visit Vegas twice a year, for four weeks at a time. A former nurse, she's on a limited budget, but doesn't like to be reminded of it while she's on vacation, so her magic words are "quarters" and "cheap," or best of all, "free." Her favorite haunts are the Westward Ho, the Frontier, and the Four Queens. While the cash rebates are small (or non-existent), these clubs are generous with food and room comps, as well as other intangible benefits for long-time members. Beth happens to be an expert-level video poker player and these casinos have an excellent selection of her favorite quarter machines, such as full-pay and loose deuces.

In order to get the maximum number of free nights, Beth and Phil have separate accounts. They make sure that their trips extend from the last two weeks of one month through the first two weeks of another. Since her A-list clubs offer two free nights per month per member, Beth and Phil qualify for four nights per month, which adds up to eight free nights each visit. Of course, the Windsors have to move a couple of times during their four-week stay, but that's a small price to pay for a month's worth of free rooms.

Beth's advice: "Read everything you can—the newspapers, the casino newsletters, the freebie magazines. Every day you'll find another special deal."

Prominent Pro

Fred Kelly lives to play video poker. He also lives off of it. If the casino doesn't have full-pay deuces wild, he can't even remember its name. In fact, Fred will not play any machine or table game unless he calculates that he can earn a minimum theoretical profit of $10 per hour. (He includes any cash rebates in that equation, but not food comps.)

Fred plays 8-10 hours a day, five days a week, and brings home a good year's pay. He takes advantage of every special promotion in town, assuming it's to his mathematical advantage, even if it means showing up to play at 4 in the morning. By combining several specials in one casino, he has managed, at times, to make more than $2,500 per week for several weeks running.

His living expenses are low, especially food costs; Freddie claims he hasn't paid for a meal in a Las Vegas casino in more than two years.

A true professional, Fred is averse to divulging anything about his favorite casinos, but he does pass along one bit of advice. "If a casino is offering a really exciting promotion, such as double-pay for royal flushes on Thursdays, get to the casino by 11 p.m. Wednesday at the latest to get a good machine."

California Dreamer

Jeanne King visits Las Vegas at least four times a year, usually on warm three-day weekends, and always with a friend who plays slot machines. That way Jeanne can double up her points and get the comps she's after. She usually stays at The Mirage, the Flamingo, or Caesars Palace, and spends more time by the pool than in the room. During the winter (i.e. non-pool) months, Jeanne carefully checks her mail and the ads in the *Los Angeles Sunday Times* "Calendar" section for specials and (especially) double-point days.

Jeanne plays quarter and dollar slots. She always gets the casino rate and never aspires to a completely comped room, which requires four times more play. Once or twice during her trip, she asks a (male) slot host to comp a dinner for two, usually at the coffee shop or buffet. Inexpensive but spacious lodgings, lots of sun, one or two free meals, and a $50 cash rebate (to pay for the gas to and from L.A.) are Jeanne's idea of the perfect three-day getaway.

Jeanne's advice: "Always insist that anyone you bring along on the trip uses your slot card. My dream is to find a friend I can talk into playing $100 slot machines with his money and my card." Good luck!

Envelope Pushers

Herbie and Rose Havoc are retired and very comfortable. They have a timeshare on the Las Vegas Strip and a large home in Massachusetts. Herbie, a retired MIT professor, is a computer expert. Though his investment income is in the six figures, he loves to beat the casinos at quarter video poker. He picks out a certain machine (usually at the Sahara, Fremont, or Four Queens), makes up a little chart showing the best plays for every hand, and camps out at the machine, confident in his system. Rose, on the other hand, keeps switching, which can be a problem if there are only four good machines in the casino. (She tries to remember to check her countdown before changing and make sure that her card is properly inserted into the new machine.)

Herbie and Rose will do anything to avoid paying for a meal in Las Vegas, including eating at buffets patronized almost exclusively by Pepto-Bismol stockholders. If they hear that $500 worth of action will earn them that free buffet, they will demand it before putting in $501. Slot hosts hate them. Rose cannot understand why fellow player Donna Flowers (next up) gets better comps for less play.

Herbie and Rose also make a game of circumventing income taxes. By playing quarters they avoid receiving a W-2G (the IRS form for a casino to report a customer's winnings). If, due to bad luck, they win a jackpot higher than $1,200 (the minimum slot win for a W-2G), they scour the local race books for betting slips or employ any other crackbrain scheme to offset their winnings (and save, at most, $350 in taxes). Unfortunately, they tell their friends (and even casual acquaintances) what they do. Herbie and Rose are really nice people at heart, so I plan to visit them every so often when they are invited to vacation at a federal facility.

The Havoc's advice? You don't need to hear it.

JC's A's AND B's

As a frequent player, I constantly refer to my A and B lists to decide where I want to play and why. For a slot club to be on my A list, it must meet all the following criteria.

- The casino must have 9/6 jacks machines at both the $1 and $5 levels. I don't play quarters. And I don't play deuces wild or double bonus machines.
- The casino must have good restaurants and easy-to-obtain food comps.
- The total rebate (cash + comps + intangibles) must be greater than 1%.
- The slot club must be user friendly. "Don't ask, won't tell"? Fine, I won't play.

These are the things that are important to me. If I played quarter deuces wild, wanted to combine video poker and blackjack play, or needed free hotel rooms, this list would be very different.

My A list—Desert Inn, Flamingo, Golden Nugget, Sam's Town, San Remo.

My B list—After each choice, I have stated not only why a casino is on my B list, but why it is not on my A list.

- Barbary Coast. My goal is a comp at Michael's restaurant. I play only during bonus times.
- Caesars Palace. This club offers high cash rebates, plus good comps and $1 9/6 jacks. What it doesn't have is $5 9/6 jacks with full slot club credit.
- Excalibur. Circus Circus clubs offer a small .25% cash rebate and are stingy with food comps, but once in a while I spend an evening at the Royal Pavilion Bar playing the $1 9/6-4700 machines.)
- Fiesta. This casino, located near my home, has great video poker. The slot club could be a bit more generous.
- The Mirage. The flip side of Caesars' club. Great $5 machines, poor $1 machines.
- Rio. I make an exception on my "don't ask, won't tell" policy, long enough to get a line pass for the buffet.

One characteristic common to both lists is that they change a lot. When the Desert Inn added $1 9/6 jacks, I added it to my A list. Both Palace and Boulder Stations were on my B list until they announced that they were dropping their buy-in logbooks for a secretive system.

It'll be interesting to compare these lists with the lists that are current at the end of 1996.

Slot Club Wizard

Every January 2, Donna Flowers boards a plane from Cleveland to Las Vegas for her annual two-month visit with her son. An avid quarter slot player, Donna partakes four to six hours a week at several different casinos, including the Fremont, Gold Coast, and Sam's Town. Donna not only knows the names of her slot hosts, she remembers their spouse's names, how many children they have, even their golf scores, which is a little out of character, as she always forgets to pack her slot cards and has to get a duplicate every time she plays. At Thanksgiving she sends her hosts holiday cards (with personal notes) and always brings them homemade gifts. On several occasions, Donna has referred other players to her hosts, resulting in a heap of goodwill.

When Donna arrives to play, she asks the change girl (after tipping her modestly) to send over her host. After chatting with Donna for five minutes or so, the host asks where she wants to go for lunch and writes up the comp—by now a ritual of Donna's own creation. After lunch, Donna plays for a couple of hours. More often than not, she orders an extra dessert to go and gives it to the host on her way out the door.

Donna reads her newsletters carefully and takes full advantage of any 55+ programs. Though her birthday is in August, her hosts have arranged that the annual birthday gifts she receives from the slot clubs may be used during her winter visits. At the end of her Las Vegas vacation, she uses her cash rebates to buy presents for her family back home and to treat her son to a gourmet meal.

Donna, a former waitress, offers this advice: "Please remember to tip your foodserver 15%-20% of the cost of the meal, even when you are comped. Stiffs are regularly reported back to the hosts, and besides, it is the casino and not the waitress who is comping your meal."

QUESTIONS AND ANSWERS

Finally, since I will not (and cannot) answer the question, "What's the best slot club?" I'll address a few other questions that most players ask.

Which slot clubs have the highest cash rebates?

The Desert Inn gives a full 1% cash rebate to both slot and video poker players, while Caesars Palace, Las Vegas Hilton, Riviera, and Lady Luck give at least 1% to slot players only. To review the procedures for figuring slot club cash rebates, see page 39. Also, note that cash-rebate percentages are subject to change.

Which clubs offer the best meal comps, where the comps are fairly easy to obtain and the food is good?

Locals casinos are always better for food comps than either downtown or the Strip. Check out Sam's Town, Boomtown, and San Remo. The Rio offers great food, but getting a comp can be more difficult than at the other joints, because it's on a time system (see page 24).

Where can I get a free hotel room?

If your goal is to sleep for free on the Strip, aim your sights at the older properties located at the north end, including the Frontier, Sahara, Stardust, Riviera, and Westward Ho. Once you become a regular customer, you should receive complimentary room offers on a regular basis.

Which club is best for quarter video poker play?

On the Strip head first to the Frontier (for deuces and double bonus) and Caesars Palace and the Flamingo (for jacks). My downtown choice for quarters is the Four Queens (all games). Locals (or tourists with cars) should drive to Sam's Town or the Fiesta.

Which club is best for dollar play?

Because of the high cash-back, good intangibles, and the availability of 9/6 jacks, I vote for the Desert Inn, Caesars Palace, Treasure Island, and the Golden Nugget. Skillful (and rich) players will like the double bonus machines at the Four Queens and the $5 deuces wild at the Frontier.

Which slot clubs count nickel play?

The following slot clubs will give some form of slot club benefit for nickel play: Bally's, Barbary Coast, Boomtown, California, Fiesta, Flamingo, Fremont, Gold Coast, Hard Rock, Imperial Palace, Jerry's Nugget, Lady Luck, Nevada Palace, Rio, Riviera, Sam's Town, San Remo, Santa Fe, Showboat, Tom's Sunset, Tropicana, and Westward Ho. For the best nickel play, check out the California, Fiesta, Fremont, Lady Luck, Sam's Town, and Westward Ho.

Do any of the casino bars offer slot club credit and good video poker?

The Flamingo has $1 9/6 jacks at bars equipped with slot card readers. The Royal Pavilion bar at Excalibur has 3-coin $1 9/6 jacks and 5-coin 9/6-4700 jacks, both with slot club. Quarter players should check out the 9/6-4700 jacks games at the Lady Luck, while $1 double bonus experts should go directly to the La Piazza bar at Caesars Palace. The Frontier has 9/6 jacks with double pay for four 7s available in $1 and $5 denominations at its bar.

Though the Holy Cow! Casino promotes a "slot club," it offers nothing more than a bonus payout for certain types of hands. The Holy Cow! bar is a great spot to meet both tourists and locals, but the video poker selection is poor.

C'mon! What's the best slot club?

In the ratings that follow, the slot clubs at Caesars Palace, Desert Inn, Sam's Town, San Remo, Four Queens, and the Golden Nugget get the highest scores, but in the final analysis, the best slot club is the one that best serves your needs, and the only way to find it is to shop around. In Chapter 9, I've provided a one-page analysis of every slot club in Las Vegas. Read each one and see what appeals to you. Whatever or however you gamble, there's a slot club that will make your casino experience more rewarding.

I hope to see you at your favorite slot club booth someday, or better yet, in the VIP line for the buffet.

Rating the Slot Clubs
of Las Vegas

What follows is a detailed description and my personal rating of every slot club in Las Vegas. The next chapter contains my recommendations for slot clubs found in Jean, Laughlin, and Mesquite.

As this book was prepared for press in October 1995, there were changes almost weekly that affected the information in this chapter. Some were major, such as a new casino (Texas) or slot club (Aladdin, Boulder Station, Palace Station), while some were minor, but still important (Caesars Palace eliminated temporary membership). I'd wager that there will be several more changes over the coming months, but by now you should know enough about the slot club scene to recognize and evaluate each change.

In each review, I've tried to give an honest appraisal of both the casino and the slot club. My best friends and worst enemies tell me that I am very opinionated. I agree, with no apologies. The purpose of this book, and particularly this section, is to give you as much background as possible on each slot club in Las Vegas. That would be impossible in the space available without being concise and at times a bit blunt.

Other writers on the Las Vegas beat, as well as some readers, will no doubt disagree with my feelings toward one casino or another. Just because I'm not wild about a particular place should not be a reason to avoid it, especially if you've had positive experiences there.

Each club's rating is a product of individual scores in four categories: its benefits, the user-friendliness of its system, the overall quality of the casino, and the video poker machines' payback percentages. (As mentioned in Chapter 5, it's impossible to rate slot machines, though one could assume that casinos offering better-paying video poker machines also offer better slots.)

Each category has a rating that is independent of the other categories. If the casino has great slot club benefits and offers lousy video poker, then it received a four-star rating (★★★★) for benefits and one star (★) for video poker. I arrived at the Overall Score by adding up the individual ratings and dividing by four.

Thus, this system assigns equal weight to all four categories: benefits, user-friendliness, video poker, and casino quality. If you feel that one criterion, such as benefits, is more important than the other three, then you might want to create your own formula based on your individual preferences.

Note that no slot club obtained an four-star overall rating, though several got 3-1/2 stars. One casino owner (who will remain unidentified) stated that it would cost him too much to get *my* four-star rating. As this book was written with players foremost in mind, I consider that a compliment.

In each review, I have listed the video poker schedules that are available. This list is not a complete inventory, as every casino has many more video poker machines than mentioned; I'm only concerned with the best ones.

The following abbreviations are used:

9/6 jacks—jacks or better machine paying 9 for a full house, 6 for a flush and 4,000 coins for a royal flush with five coins played. Expert play yields a 99.5% return.

9/6-4700—same as above, but pays 4,700 coins for a royal flush. Expert play yields a 99.9% return.

8/5 jacks progressive—same as above, but pays only 8 for a full house and 5 for a flush. Progressive jackpots begin at 4,000 coins and increase until someone hits a royal flush. The breakeven royal flush jackpot is 8,800 coins ($2,200 for quarter machines). Expert play yields a 97.3% return at 4,000 coins.

8/5 bonus—a version of jacks or better that pays more for certain four-of-a-kinds. Four 2s, 3s, or 4s pays 40, four aces pays 80, and all other four-of-a-kinds pays the standard 25. Expert play yields a 99.2% return.

8/5 aces and faces—a version of 8/5 bonus where four kings, queens, or jacks pays 40, four aces pays 80, and all other four-of-a-kinds pays 25. Expert play yields a 99.3% return.

10/7 double bonus—double bonus poker pays only 1 for two pair, but a lot more for quads. The schedule for this game is: jacks or better 1, two pair 1, three-of-a-kind 3, straight 5, flush 7, full house 10, four 5s through kings 50, four 2s, 3s, or 4s 80, and four aces 160. Though the payback is 100.2%, this game should not be attempted unless you play at a professional level and have worked out an accurate strategy, preferably with a computer.

full-pay (classic) deuces—deuces wild paying according to the following schedule: three-of-a-kind 1, straight or flush 2, full house 3, four-of-a-kind 5, straight flush 9, five-of-a-kind 15, wild royal flush 25, four deuces 200, royal flush 800. Expert play yields a 100.7% return.

loose deuces—same as above except that four-of-a-kind pays 4, straight flush pays 10, and four deuces pays 500. Expert play yields a 101% return.

bonus deuces—a variety of deuces wild found at Sam's Town. Three-of-a-kind pays 1, straight 2, flush 3, full house 4, four-of-a-kind 4, straight flush 10, five-of-a-kind 10, wild royal flush 20, four deuces 400, royal flush 800. Expert play yields a 100.9% return.

sequential—several of the above games have bonuses for sequential royal flushes. A sequential royal is AKQJT or TJQKA in those specific orders. Some sequentials pay one way, others pay two ways. The amount of the sequential bonuses varies from casino to casino. The most common sequential is $12,500 for quarters. It raises the return percentage by .2% when paid only one way and .4% when paid two ways. Example: 9/6 jacks (99.5%) with a two-way sequential (.4%) returns 99.9%.

Not to belabor a point, but things change all the time, and the changes we are seeing in Las Vegas video poker inventory are usually not for the better. The best sources for up-to-date information on new developments are the *Las Vegas Advisor* (see the back of this book) and Dan Paymar's *Video Poker Times* (2540 S. Maryland Parkway #141, Las Vegas, NV 89109; $45 for six issues).

Jacks or Better			
	9/6	9/6-4700	8/5 prog.
Royal flush (max. coins)	800	940	800-2,200
Straight flush	50	50	50
Four-of-a-kind	25	25	25
Full house	9	9	8
Flush	6	6	5
Straight	4	4	4
Three-of-a-kind	3	3	3
Two pair	2	2	2
Jacks or better	1	1	1
Payback %	**99.5%**	**99.9%**	**97.3%-100%+**

Deuces Wild

	Classic	Loose	Bonus
Royal flush (max. coins)	800	800	800
Four deuces	200	500	400
Wild royal	25	25	20
Five-of-a-kind	15	15	10
Straight flush	9	10	10
Four-of-a-kind	5	4	4
Full house	3	3	4
Flush	2	2	3
Straight	2	2	2
Three-of-a-kind	1	1	1
Payback %	**100.7%**	**101.0%**	**100.9%**

Bonus Poker

	8/5 Bonus	8/5 Aces & Faces	10/7 Double Bonus
Royal flush (max. coins)	800	800	800
Straight flush	50	50	50
Four aces	80	80	160
Four Ks, Qs, Js	25	40	50
Four 5s-10s	25	25	50
Four2s, 3s, 4s	40	25	80
Full house	8	8	10
Flush	5	5	7
Straight	4	4	4
Three-of-a-kind	3	3	3
Two pair	2	2	1
Jacks or better	1	1	1
Payback %	**99.2%**	**99.3%**	**100.2%**

Aladdin Hotel & Casino
Prestige Membership Club (not rated)
3667 Las Vegas Blvd. S.
(702) 736-0111
(800) 367-2850

For many years, the Aladdin seemed to be a "kiss-of-death" casino (like the now-defunct El Rancho, Dunes, and Landmark). Since its official opening on January 1, 1966, the property has seen bankruptcy, mob investigations, Wayne Newton, Elvis and Priscilla, and absentee Japanese ownership.

Within the last year, new management seems to have learned the magic words ("abracadabra" and "alakazaam"?) and the Aladdin is finally beginning to look and feel like a winner. The casino is much cleaner, more crowded, and the staff more upbeat than I have ever seen here. A friend of mine and regular Las Vegas visitor who recently stayed there raved about his room. This could be "a whole new world" for the Aladdin and its customers.

The Aladdin initiated a computerized player tracking system in late summer 1995, replacing its old manual time system. Even though you can sign up and get a card, the system is very much in its infancy. I'm unable to provide an analysis of the club at this time, because the slot club staff was still working out the bugs as this book went to press. From all appearances, it will be a "don't ask, won't tell" secretive system.

I can tell you that the Aladdin does not have a strong inventory of video poker machines. The only mildly interesting machines are a few quarter 8/5 jacks progressives. I will reserve any judgment until the system is fully operational.

Optimal Strategy: If you're making the trek from Tropicana to Flamingo, stop in and sign-up, but wait and see how the slot club works before putting any serious money into the Aladdin's so-so machines.

Bally's Las Vegas
MVP Club (★1/2)
3645 Las Vegas Blvd. S.
(702) 739-4561
(800) 722-5597

Bally's is the closest thing to an Atlantic City casino you'll find in southern Nevada. That's not a compliment. Though the rooms are large and the restaurants above average, the place has an uncomfortable corporate feel to it.

There's not a single decent video poker machine in the entire casino. The MVP Club awards both cash and comps equal to 30% of the casino's theoretical win on a one-third cash and two-thirds comp basis. For example, if you play $1 8/5 jacks video poker for one hour, your theoretical loss is calculated at about $80. The MVP club will rebate $8 in cash and $16 in comps. In many other Strip casinos the same action returns considerably more. (For example, one hour of $1 video poker at Caesars Palace across the street earns a $20 rebate and an additional $20 in comps.)

The MVP Club is also hard to work with. To begin with, the card readers do not disclose your point totals. To find out what your benefits are, you must use one of the club's special point readers located on the casino floor. Or you can go to the slot desk, where the staff is efficient but rather cold. Either way, you have no way of knowing what your play is really earning or how to increase your benefits. The entire process lacks western hospitality and common sense.

Four times a year, club members receive *Bally's Winner*, an attractive four-color booklet detailing upcoming entertainment and special events. A careful reading usually reveals a decent room and show offer. Also, the MVP Club has been helpful in securing good seats to Bally's shows or to the popular Sunday brunch.

Benefits ★   User Friendly ★★   Video Poker ★
Casino Rating ★★★   Overall Score ★1/2

Optimal Strategy: Sign up and put a half-hour's worth of quarter action into a machine to get on the list for *Bally's Winner*. Monitor offers you receive in the mail.

Barbary Coast Hotel & Casino
Fun Club (★★1/2)
3595 Las Vegas Blvd. S.
(702) 737-7111
(800) 634-6755

All but surrounded by the Flamingo Hilton, the Barbary Coast stands at the corner of Flamingo Ave. and Las Vegas Boulevard. While some might appreciate its low-key atmosphere and "old Vegas" feel, many more find the Barbary Coast to be just plain unfriendly. Experienced blackjack players tell me that if you win three hands in a row, you'll look up to find half the staff is staring at you. Win five and you risk being asked to leave.

Recently though, the casino has been making an effort to make slot customers feel welcome. On my last few visits, the staff seemed especially friendly and I received several meal comps.

The Fun Club is a scaled-down version of the club found at the Gold Coast, Barbary's sister casino. While both clubs award points based on a coin-out formula (approximately .2% of whatever you win), the Barbary Coast does not have Gold Coast's elaborate four-color prize-redemption catalog. Don't despair; you can apply Barbary Coast points at the Gold Coast (other than food and gift certificates). Neither club gives cash rebates.

Most of the items on the Barbary Coast prize list are either monogrammed items or meal comps. Dinner at McDonald's is 1,250 points (or $1,250 in winnings), while dinner at Michael's, the Barbary's ultra-gourmet room, is 23,750 points. The Barbary Coast holds frequent double- and triple-point days, much more often, in fact, than the Gold Coast. The system is easy to use. You can check total points at every machine.

Video poker machine inventory seems, of late, to be changing for the worse. (In order to pay for the increased number of comps?) Available in rapidly decreasing numbers are quarter 8/5 progressives, 9/6 jacks, and 9/6 double bonus progressives, dollar 9/6 jacks, and for big nickel players 9/5 jacks progressives.

Benefits ★★★   User Friendly ★★★   Video Poker ★★
Casino Rating ★★   Overall Score ★★1/2

Optimal Strategy: Want a fabulous and free meal at one of the town's premier restaurants? Wait for triple-point periods, play a dollar 9/6 jacks machine for five hours, or five dollar 9/5 jacks progressive for one hour (if the jackpot is higher than $25,000). You will earn a dinner for two at Michael's that you will never forget.

Boomtown Hotel Casino & RV Resort
Player's Club (★★★)
3333 Blue Diamond Road
(702) 263-7777
(800) 588-7711

Boomtown, located south of the Strip off Interstate 15, is a friendly casino. A very friendly casino. I go there a lot and have never encountered an employee who was the least bit rude or abrupt. One reason everyone is so friendly is that this the only Las Vegas casino where dealers keep their own tips instead of pooling them, thus friendlier-than-average dealers choose to work here.

Opened in 1994 with a country-western theme, Boomtown is a favorite of both locals and tourists, especially those who drive recreational vehicles and use the hotel's fine RV park. (Active slot club members receive extra considerations at the RV park.) Though dining selections are limited to a buffet and coffee shop, both serve up good food at reasonable prices. Thursdays through Sundays, the casino opens the Opera House ballroom for a special all-you-can-eat chicken and rib feast.

The Players Club offers a cash rebate of .49% for slots and .19% for video poker via a coin-in point system. In lieu of cash, points can be used to acquire mugs, T-shirts, jackets, etc. with the Boomtown logo. The card should also be shown when playing keno, bingo, or any table game. The system is user-friendly: a player can check both total points and countdown from all machines. From time to time, the club schedules double time.

Boomtown is generous with intangibles. On several occasions while cashing in points, I've been offered a food comp without having to ask. In my experience, a player will receive a buffet comp for two for $7,000 of video poker action or $3,000 on slots.

The better video poker machines at Boomtown include quarter 8/5 bonus jacks, full-pay deuces, and 10/7 double bonus. At the fifty-cent and dollar levels, you will find 8/5 bonus, 10/7 double bonus, and 9/6 jacks. There is also a high-roller area with 8/5 bonus and 9/6 jacks.

Benefits ★★★   User Friendly ★★★★   Video Poker ★★★
Casino Rating ★★   Overall Score ★★★

Optimal Strategy: Play either quarter deuces or the fifty-cent 9/6 jacks or 10/7 double bonus, especially during bonus time. Every time you accrue 170 points, pick up a $5 rebate check and ask for a food comp at the coffee shop or buffet.

Boulder Station
Boarding Pass (not rated)
4111 Boulder Highway
(702) 456-7777
(800) 634-6371

When Boulder Station opened its doors in August 1994, many thought it would be an exact duplicate of Palace Station. They were wrong. Though Boulder Station did duplicate the finer points of its older sister, such as the wonderful buffet and friendly atmosphere, it unveiled them in one of the classiest casinos in Las Vegas. Strategically located at the intersection of Boulder Highway and US 93/95, Boulder Station features polished wood floors, an open-air setting complete with sky art above, and a very logical casino floor plan. For example, table games are placed in the middle of the casino, far away from the traffic flow.

The staff here is extremely friendly and professional. I know of few places I'd rather spend an afternoon.

Station Casinos has announced that as of November 1995, they will completely abandon their buy-in log-book method of rating and comping players. In its place will be a computerized tracking system, known as the Boarding Pass, similar to the club at the newest Station property, Texas. According to various casino sources, the three casinos' systems will eventually be blended into one, so players can earn comps at one casino and spend them at another.

I will reserve judgment until the Boarding Pass system is completely operational. Station Casinos is competing in the tough local market, so one can expect some early fits and starts.

As with Palace Station, video poker machine inventory changes often as management is quick to remove an unprofitable machine. For now, the best of the lot are several quarter and dollar 8/5 bonus poker sequentials, 10/7 double bonus, and 9/6 double bonus sequential progressives.

Optimal Strategy: Boulder Station is worth a visit just to see the decor and enjoy the good food and service. Once the Boarding Pass system is up and running, stop by, join the club, play for an hour or so, and see what develops.

Caesars Palace
Emperors Club (★★★1/2)
3570 Las Vegas Blvd. S.
(702) 731-7110
(800) 722-2727

No name conjures up Las Vegas glitz and glamour more readily than Caesars Palace, and the Emperors Club is one of the best slot clubs in Las Vegas.

Quarter slot players receive cash rebates of .80%, dollar action is rewarded with a full 1%. Video poker is .40% and .67% for quarter and dollars, respectively. Additional meal comps, as well as various room discounts, can be obtained through the slot hosts.

The Emperors Club is easy to understand. Countdown and total points are displayed at all times. There are two booths, both well staffed. Though you must earn 200 points before receiving your first cash rebate of $20, the club no longer requires any play to be granted full membership.

Two intangibles stand out. Many of the pricey Forum Shops, including Babe and Field of Dreams, offer a 10% discount to Emperors Club members. Even better, the club occasionally mails postcards offering two free tickets to the headliner shows in the Circus Maximus showroom, including Julio Iglesias, Natalie Cole, and David Copperfield. Quite a benefit.

Caesars has recently installed the "Request" system. Club members are issued a second card allowing them to convert their Emperors Club points into credits without ever leaving the machine. If you want cash for your points, you still have to go to the club booth.

9/6 jacks and 8/5 bonus can be found at the quarter and dollar levels. Quarter 10/7 double bonus machines can be found in the La Piazza bar. Avoid the $5 machines, as you have to choose between 8/5 jacks with a poor 97.5% cash-back or 9/6 jacks that only return a low .20% cash rebate. For some reason, the casino offers Chicken Caesar to their big nickel players.

Benefits ★★★★   User Friendly ★★★★   Video Poker ★★
Casino Rating ★★★★   Overall Score ★★★1/2

Optimal Strategy: Except for deuces wild players, everyone will find their game here and be well rewarded. The best bet is dollar 9/6 jacks which, combined with the slot club reward, allows experts to play with a 100.1% return. Comps, mail-out offers, and other intangibles then become rich frosting on an exquisite cake. Hail Caesars!

California Hotel & Casino
Cal Club (★★1/2)
12 Ogden Avenue
(702) 385-1222
(800) 634-6255

The California was the Boyd Group's first Las Vegas casino, the first of many. Located downtown, a bit off the beaten Fremont path, the California heavily markets and caters to Hawaiians, which gives the property a definite island atmosphere. Two years ago, the Boyds purchased the defunct Main Street Station across the street and are slowly renovating the structure.

The Cal Club pays a straight .10% cash rebate based on coin-in on all slots and video poker machines, including nickels. The club occasionally schedules bonus times. As with other Boyd properties, the main benefit of this club is the availability of comps through the slot hosts. Knowledgeable players, as well as personal experience, tell me that the hosts are much more generous to hotel guests, especially those from their target market, than to locals or guests from other non-Boyd hotels. When you connect with a host, a good choice for your first comp is the Pasta Pirate, one of my favorite Italian restaurants.

Players can check their points, but not the countdown, from any machine in the casino. The club publishes a four-color newsletter, 90% of which is pictures of winners. Unfortunately, I find the slot club booth to be seriously understaffed (the help is doing double duty running daily mini-tournaments), thus service can be abrupt. Also, when you call the hotel and ask for the Cal Club, you're connected with a snack bar of the same name.

The California offers excellent video poker, including quarter 8/5 bonus, 9/6 jacks, full-pay and loose deuces, and 10/7 double-bonus. Dollar machines include 8/5 bonus, 9/6 jacks, and 10/7 double bonus.

Benefits ★★   User Friendly ★★   Video Poker ★★★★
Casino Rating ★★★   Overall Score ★★1/2

Optimal Strategy: The California puts together excellent airfare-hotel packages for Hawaiians, which anyone coming from the 50th state should check out. The rest of us should scout out one of the good video poker machines, run about $2,000 through it, then call over a slot host. Ask about dinner for two at the Pasta Pirate.

Circus Circus Hotel & Casino
Ringmaster Club (★★1/2)
2880 Las Vegas Blvd. S.
(702) 734-0410
(800) 344-5252

Whether Circus Circus is first or last on your casino ratings list (it's always one or the other), no one can deny that the entire operation is extremely well-run. The casino boasts a vast array of attractions, including Las Vegas' first carnival midway, a five-acre indoor amusement park complete with the world's largest indoor roller coaster, and even the dignified Steakhouse.

The Ringmaster Club pays a straightforward .25% cash rebate on all slot and video poker machines. In lieu of cash, points can be used to obtain free meals or logoed items. For example, for 280 points ($2,800 coin-in) you get a choice of either $7 in cash, $23 in free buffet meals, or a quality T-shirt worth about $20 retail. Do not redeem your points for a Steakhouse meal. You will not receive a comp, but instead will get $40 in scrip for the same number of points needed to receive $40 cash.

Players must earn 200 points ($2,000 coin-in) to obtain full membership, which includes the casino rate on a room and special reservations number. You can check the countdown and points from any machine and the staff here is especially helpful. Though the Ringmaster Club does not have a newsletter, it sends out frequent promotional mail, usually for slot tournaments.

Serious video poker players will find nothing of interest at Circus Circus. The best quarter games are 8/5 bonus and there's a handful of scattered dollar 8/5 progressives. Also be aware that children run wild in this casino. If you don't like kids (or just don't like kids in casinos), go elsewhere. If, on the other hand, you are a Circus Circus fan, then consider taking your play next door to Slots A Fun. Not only are there fewer distractions, but the video poker machines are much better (9/6 jacks at both the quarter and dollar levels) and the slot clubs at Circus Circus and Slots A Fun are one and the same.

Benefits ★★   User Friendly ★★★   Video Poker ★★
Casino Rating ★★★   Overall Score ★★1/2

Optimal Strategy: Join the Ringmaster Club at Circus Circus, then go over to Slots A Fun and pick out a good 9/6 jacks video poker machine. Run up 300 points ($3,000 coin-in) and redeem them for several buffets or the excellent T-shirt.

Desert Inn Hotel, Casino & Spa
Celebrity Club (★★★1/2)
3145 Las Vegas Blvd. S.
(702) 733-4345
(800) 634-6909

Once the residence of Howard Hughes and Dan Tanna (as in "Vega$"), the Desert Inn caters to high rollers in an atmosphere of quiet elegance. First-timers are quite surprised when they see how small the casino is, about one-tenth the size of the MGM Grand.

The Celebrity Club, which opened in early 1995, fits right in with the casino's low-key ambience. This club doesn't have a booth; it operates from several elegant desks unobtrusively located on the west wall of the casino. You're invited to sit down while a well-dressed employee fills out the forms, as if you were opening a new money-market account.

The best part of this story is the club's generous cash rebates. The Celebrity Club pays .67% on quarters and 1% on dollars for both slots and video poker. You'll be offered restaurant scrip in the same amount, but there is no reason to go that route. Cash can also be used at the restaurants, not to mention many other places on the planet.

Total points and countdown are displayed at all machines. Though the staff tries to be helpful, the computer age is new to the Desert Inn and not all the employees understand the system.

Though management states that the cash rebate is the entire benefit from the club, the slot hosts do write dinner and show comps for heavy slot action. Use the usual strategy to try for intangibles. The worst they can say is no (you'll still get the nice rebate). Until recently the Desert Inn's major downside was the poor selection of video poker machines. New dollar 9/6 jacks and quarter 8/5 bonus have improved the situation immensely.

Benefits ★★★★   User Friendly ★★★★   Video Poker ★★★
Casino Rating ★★★   Overall Score ★★★1/2

Optimal Strategy: The Desert Inn gives the largest video poker cash rebate in Nevada. Skilled players can achieve a payback of 100% or better, as long as they stick to the dollar 9/6 machines. Warning: Anyone attempting long-term play on the $5 machines should have a total bankroll of at least $100,000.

Excalibur Hotel & Casino
Crown Club (★★1/2)
3850 Las Vegas Blvd. S.
(702) 597-7417
(800) 879-1379

Excalibur was the first megaresort to seriously go after the family business. Operated efficiently and effectively by Circus Circus, the casino has friendly dealers, low-minimum table games, excellent learning tables for live poker, a video arcade, and a knights-in-shining-armor show that is as entertaining as it is hokey. I always have a good time there.

The Crown Club gives a cash rebate of .25%, based on coin-in on both slot and video poker play. Once you sign up, you have a maximum of seven days to earn 400 points ($4,000 play). You then receive $10 and a permanent card. The Crown Club does not offer bonus times and the cards are not valid for anything at the tables. Players can check total points and the countdown at every machine.

Besides the cash rebate, this is a good place for intangibles. In my experience, $2,500 worth of play will get you a buffet for two, while $5,000 in action will treat you and a guest to an excellent prime rib and Yorkshire pudding at Sir Galahad's. Unfortunately, casino hosts are often hard to find; the casino seems to employ only one per shift, and Excalibur is a very large casino. (In one instance I was told that no one was available because "the host had to run home.") I've also noticed that the hosts only write a comps for the day of the play, or on occasion, the day after.

Several 9/6 jacks machines are scattered throughout Excalibur, but you have to search for them. Good quarter machines border the sports book, while five-coin dollar 9/6-4700 jacks and three-coin dollar 9/6-4000 jacks can be found at the circular Royal Pavilion bar. Players should also check out the quarter, fifty-cent, and dollar 8/5 bonus poker machines.

Benefits ★★   User Friendly ★★★   Video Poker ★★
Casino Rating ★★★★   Overall Score ★★1/2

Optimal Strategy: Head to the Royal Pavilion bar, chat with the friendly bartenders, and play the three- or five-coin dollar 9/6 jacks machines. The five-coin machines with a royal flush jackpot of $4,700, combined with the Crown Club rebate, give you a 100.2% payback, and you get free drinks to boot.

Fiesta Casino Hotel
Amigo Club (★★★)
2400 N. Rancho Dr., North Las Vegas
(702) 631-7000
(800 731-7333

The Fiesta was the second casino built on Rancho Drive (after the Santa Fe) to service the exploding northwest residential market. The operation started small, but has already added a state-of-the-art sports and race book complete with easy chairs, individual televisions, and even a drive-up betting window.

The Fiesta takes pride in its vast selection of full-pay (and better) video poker. Management considers the Amigo Club a small perk for its steady customers. There are no cash rebates; members can use points earned (via coin-in) toward free meals or to acquire logoed items in the gift shop. Depending on how you apply your points, the club benefits add about .15% to your total payback.

A quick analysis of the prize list shows that points go farther when spent on the buffet. Though the Fiesta restaurants are quite good, I would not use my points for a sit-down dinner comp unless I planned to eat a very substantial meal. (Dinner for two at the Southwestern restaurant, Garduño's, requires $12,500 play. That same action will get you six dinner buffets.)

Players can use the card anywhere in the casino, including all machines (nickels too), all table games, keno, bingo, and the race and sports book. The casino recently installed the best card readers in Las Vegas, featuring a continually updated display of total points, session points, and countdown. Its excellent newsletter is filled with specials, twofers, and an easy-to-read promotions calendar.

The Fiesta's best attribute is its quarter video poker, including 8/5 bonus, 9/6 progressives, full-pay deuces progressives, and 9/7 double bonus progressives. Dollar selection includes 9/6 jacks progressives and 10/7 double bonus progressives. Truly skilled double bonus players (with very deep pockets) should check out the $5 10/7 double bonus machine.

Benefits ★★   User Friendly ★★★★   Video Poker ★★★★
Casino Rating ★★   Overall Score ★★★

Optimal Strategy: Local video poker players (especially those who live or work in northwest Las Vegas) should definitely check this club out, if for no other reason than to get the newsletter. Hint: Check the Fiesta funbook for a special bonus-point coupon before signing up.

Flamingo Hilton
Flamingo Players Club (★★★)
2555 Las Vegas Blvd. S.
(702) 733-3111
(800) 255-4882

Opened in December 1946 by mobster Bugsy Siegel, the Flamingo has been expanded and renovated so many times that it is now the fourth largest hotel in the world. The latest addition created the most attractive pool complex in Las Vegas.

The Flamingo Players Club has also made several recent changes, all for the better. Formerly a member of the secretive "don't ask, won't tell" society, the club has updated its card readers on all machines to display total "comp dollars." There's also a well-organized brochure detailing how to get comp dollars and what they buy in the hotel.

The club rebates scrip equal to .58% for quarter play, .67% for $1, and .71% for $5 play. At present, video poker players receive the same benefits as slot players, though this may soon change. Comp dollars may be used for dinner in any of the restaurants, at the shows, in the health spa, or applied toward a room. The brochure gives good estimates of how many comp dollars are necessary to cover dinner for one or two at the various restaurants. For example, breakfast for one at Lindy's coffee shop runs about $7, while dinner for two at the Beef Baron steakhouse comes in at around $70. Ask the booth to issue a comp for the amount suggested in the brochure. All unused comp dollars are credited back to your account.

The Players Club does not issue a newsletter and does not run bonus times as of this writing. You can use your card at the tables for additional comp credit. Members recently received free and almost-free weekends (determined by playing history), including a two-night stay and two buffets.

The machine offering is good for a large Strip hotel. You will find quarter 8/5 bonus poker, and 9/6-4700 jacks, as well as dollar and five dollar 9/6 jacks. Deuces wild fans should check out the machines next door at O'Shea's, the Flamingo's low-roller casino.

Benefits ★★★   User Friendly ★★★   Video Poker ★★★
Casino Rating ★★★★   Overall Score ★★★

Optimal Strategy: The Flamingo is one of the best casino resorts on the Las Vegas Strip. Dollar video poker players putting in six-hour days can earn enough points to cover room and three meals (including an elegant dinner) and possibly a show.

Four Queens Hotel & Casino
Reel Winners Club (★★★1/2)
202 Fremont Street
(702) 385-4011
(800) 634-6045

Located downtown at the corner of Casino Center Drive and Fremont Street, the Four Queens offers good games, strong promotions, and a decent selection of restaurants, including Hugo's Cellar, one of the finest upscale eateries in Nevada.

The Reel Winners Club has been around awhile, but cash rebates were added only recently. Slot players earn a .62% cash rebate on quarter play and .50% on dollar action. Video poker players get a cash rebate of .31% on both quarter and dollar machines. Big nickel slot and video poker machines pay a .20% cash rebate. Reel Winners Club members who play blackjack should request a special card from the pit boss so table time can be credited toward room and meal comps.

The Four Queens runs some of the strongest promotions in Las Vegas (gambler's spree, win cards, video poker bingo cards), and they can increase your cash rebate and overall payback percentage.

Intangible benefits are excellent and innovative. Members with more than 200 lifetime points ($800 in quarter slot action) can stay at the Four Queens absolutely free on designated "ditch days." Members over 55 with 500+ lifetime points can attend a special monthly bingo session (16 games, jackpots $25-$300), as can any member with 5,000+ lifetime points. In my experience, a coffee shop dinner for two at Magnolia's is comped for $3,000-$4,000 in action.

The Reel Winners Club is very user friendly. Members can check both total points and countdown from any machine and booth personnel are particularly helpful. Every other month, the club mails a newsletter detailing all special events, ditch days, and other offers to members with 1,000+ points.

Among the many good video poker machines are quarter full-pay deuces, 10/7 double bonus, and 9/6 jacks. 8/5 bonus, 9/6 jacks, and 10/7 double bonus are available at the dollar level.

Benefits ★★★   User Friendly ★★★★   Video Poker ★★★★
Casino Rating ★★★   Overall Score ★★★1/2

Optimal Strategy: If you play quarter slots or video poker and visit Las Vegas often, the Four Queens is an excellent choice for long-term benefits and profit. The more you learn about this club, the better it gets.

Fremont Hotel & Casino
Five Star Slot Club (★★1/2)
200 East Fremont Street
(702) 385-3232
(800) 634-6182

The 40-year-old Fremont combines decent gambling, a distinctive downtown look, and the fine dining you expect from a Boyd casino, which acquired it from less reputable interests in 1985.

I find the name Five Star Slot Club a tad ambitious, as it pays a modest .25% for slots, and an even smaller .10% for video poker. You can do better at almost any other downtown property. Other Boyd properties usually make up for the low cash back by being generous with food comps, but the hosts at the Fremont have proven hard to work with. That's too bad, because both the Fremont buffet (especially on seafood nights) and the Second Street Grill are excellent restaurants, getting far less praise than they deserve. Unfortunately the hotel rooms haven't been upgraded for a long time.

Based on experiences at the Fremont and other Boyd casinos, I suggest connecting with a slot host after running $1,000 or so though a machine and requesting the buffet. Remember, diplomacy goes a long way.

Though you can check your points at any machine, you cannot check the countdown. The slot club booth is poorly located (in the middle of a busy aisle) and frequently understaffed.

One fun benefit of the Five Star Slot Club is its free daily slot pull. Once per day, members can insert their card into a reader on a special machine located near the slot booth. It's possible, though don't count on it, to win a big jackpot; more often than not, you get one to three special tickets. Accumulate 200 tickets and get a Fremont jacket. True, it might take a while, but it's free. (Remember, if you and your spouse have separate accounts, you can do this in half the time, then fight over who gets the jacket.)

The excellent video poker selection includes quarter 8/5 bonus, 9/6 jacks, and full-pay deuces, as well as dollar 8/5 bonus and 9/6-4500 jacks.

Benefits ★★   User Friendly ★★   Video Poker ★★★
Casino Rating ★★★   Overall Score ★★1/2

Optimal Strategy: As with other Boyd properties, your main goal is to hook up with a slot host to get a comp at one of the Fremont's excellent restaurants. Do this after playing $1,000-$2,000 through one of its high-paying machines.

Frontier Hotel & Gambling Hall
Gold Rush Club (★★★)
3120 Las Vegas Blvd. S.
(702) 794-8200
(800) 634-6966

The Frontier has been the object of a bitter long-running labor strike. You will have to cross picket lines to enter the hotel. If you do stay here, ask for a room away from Las Vegas Blvd., or your peace and quiet may be regularly interrupted by bullhorns.

The Gold Rush slot club does not pay cash, but rewards players amply with gifts, comps, and other intangibles via a two-tiered process. For every $2.50 spent on slots or $7.50 on video poker, the club awards one point, which can be used in the gift shop or beauty parlor. For every 70 points, an additional $1 comp credit is issued toward rooms and meals. (There's a limit of two "comp" rooms per month.) I calculate the above rebates to be worth .4% for video poker and 1.2% for slots. This is quite high, but it's not cash. People who get a lot of points usually wind up exchanging them for overpriced jewelry and watches in the gift shop. The casino schedules regular double-point days.

Once 1,000 points have been earned (lifetime), the player is entitled to two free "getaway" rooms per month, forever. These getaway nights are in addition to the comp nights mentioned above. Additionally, once the player has earned 2,000 points, he receives monthly coupons. These coupons vary, but typically include slot and video poker bonuses, meal deals (including buffet twofers), and free entries to slot tournaments.

Players can check points and countdown from the machines, and the club publishes one of the best newsletters around.

The Frontier has an excellent selection of video poker machines, including quarter 9/6 jacks and jacks progressives, 9/6 jacks with double pay for four 7s (100.0%), full-pay deuces, and 10/7 double bonus; dollar 9/6 jacks, 9/6 jacks with double pay for four 7s, full-pay deuces, and 10/7 double bonus, as well as $5 9/6 jacks with double pay for four 7s.

Benefits ★★★   User Friendly ★★★   Video Poker ★★★★
Casino Rating ★★   Overall Score ★★★

Optimal Strategy: Skilled video poker players looking for a steady Strip source of free food and rooms should spend time at the Frontier. This is an excellent club, with the best rewards going to the members who take full advantage of all the benefits.

Gold Coast Hotel & Casino
The Club (★★1/2)
4000 West Flamingo Road
(702) 367-7111
(800) 331-5334

This year (as in previous years) the readers of the *Las Vegas Review-Journal* voted The Club at the Gold Coast the best slot club in Las Vegas. This is quite an accomplishment for a non-cash-rebate club, even if it does cater primarily to locals. The casino is popular for its dance hall, movie theaters, and bowling alley.

Though I do not agree with the voters, I can understand their choice. The Gold Coast promotes its club with large newspaper ads, ubiquitous billboards, and extensive in-casino publicity. The continuous campaign also stresses the coin-out aspect of the system, so players who think they are lucky (and who doesn't?) feel they'll do better at the Gold Coast. The Club is also very user friendly and is big on bonus times.

The club awards one point for every dollar you win on any machine, slot or video poker, including nickels. You can redeem your points for rooms, meals, gift certificates or any of more than 100 items displayed in its redemption catalogs, including a trip to Hawaii for 875,000 points. The Club frequently runs specials such as double- and even triple-bonus times.

My experience suggests that 500 points are equal to about $1 in benefits, so you can figure that the club rebate is equal to .2%. Points will go farther when redeemed for meals or gift certificates, or used at the casino's bowling alley or movie theater, as most of the prizes are overpriced. Though the Club occasionally comps an extra meal to a big player, it doesn't happen very often.

The Gold Coast has a respectable selection of machines, including quarter 8/5 bonus jacks progressives, quarter aces & faces bonus jacks, 9/6 jacks, and full-pay deuces. At the dollar level, you will find 8/5 bonus, 8/5 progressive and, some 9/6 jacks. Avoid the $5 9/5 jacks progressive unless the jackpot is greater than $25,000. You can check your point total from any of these machines.

Benefits ★★   User Friendly ★★★★   Video Poker ★★★
Casino Rating ★★   Overall Score ★★1/2

Optimal Strategy: When you spot a Gold Coast ad for double- or triple-point periods, head to one of the full-pay machines and play away. Four hours of quarter play (and triple points) earns you four buffet dinners, 12 games of ten-pin, or a $20 gift certificate.

Golden Nugget Hotel & Casino
24 Karat Club (★★★1/2)
129 Fremont Street
(702) 385-7111
(800) 777-5687

The first casino in Steve Wynn's gambling empire, the Golden Nugget is downtown's most elegant destination. The 24 Karat Club is Las Vegas' oldest slot club and still one of the best, assuming you play dollars or higher.

The club pays a straight .67% cash rebate on all slot and video poker play, $1 and up. The manner by which you earn the points is part of the fun. The machines have ticket dispensers that display a number between 1 and 75. These numbers represent the countdown required to get the next ticket. Once you get to zero the machine resets to 75. Soooooooooo, pick your machine based on the ticket dispenser that displays the lowest number.

Each ticket is worth 50¢. You must have 30 tickets to become a permanent member and to receive your first $15 voucher and two free buffets. Members get the casino rate and unlimited line passes to the buffet. Redemption strategy from this point depends on the meal comp you're interested in (which comes in addition to your cash). I'll explain. When you turn in 40 tickets you receive $20 and two free buffets; 50 tickets gets $25 and a coffee shop comp for two; 100 tickets returns $50 and dinner for two at Stephano's. So unless you are leaving Las Vegas and not returning in the near future, do not turn in less than 40 tickets. All meal comps are issued in pairs, so bring someone along.

This system is easy to work with and the 24 Karat Club staff is helpful. They might even advise you on angles to get more comps, i.e., if you've earned an additional restaurant comp, the staff will tell you. This sort of attitude is one reason why Steve Wynn's casinos are among the most successful in the world. The best (and almost only) machines in the house to play are the $1 9/6 jacks located along the wall running from the casino toward the hotel and restaurants. There are also several decent $5 machines in the high-roller area on the Fremont side of the Golden Nugget.

Benefits ★★★★   User Friendly ★★★★   Video Poker ★★
Casino Rating ★★★★   Overall Score ★★★1/2

Optimal Strategy: Dollar players only. Find a 9/6 jacks machine with the lowest countdown number. Never cash in less than 40 tickets at a time (unless you are a new member with 30 tickets).

Hacienda Hotel & Casino
Club Viva (★★1/2)
3950 Las Vegas Blvd. S.
(702) 739-8911
(800) 843-2637

The Hacienda was the trophy in a recent dogfight between Circus Circus and its former CEO, William Bennett. Both wanted to buy it from the Sahara Corporation, not so much for the casino, but for the prime location. Circus won. Assume that Circus Circus will be making some changes within the coming year to bring the Hacienda casino and slot club more in line with its other properties.

Club Viva does not pay cash, but awards comps and prizes instead. Slot and video poker players receive one point for every $7.50 deposited in any machine. For 350 points you get a free buffet, 1,000 points gets you a $10 coupon at the New York Pasta Company. The points are worth about one penny each, a little over .13% of added return. Several times a month the casino runs double- and triple-point bonus times.

Ten nights a month (never Fridays or Saturdays) are designated as "Fiesta Days." Members who have earned 250 points since their last visit can stay at the hotel for free. Club members are also given a 10% discount on all meals in the Cactus Room Coffee Shop.

Club Viva is easy to work with; players can check points and countdown at all machines. The club produces an informative colorful newsletter for members. The Club Viva booth could use more staff and printed materials relating to prizes. Quarter video poker machine selection include 9/6 jacks, full-pay and loose deuces, 8/5 sequential bonus jacks, and 10/7 double bonus. Dollar machines are limited to a small selection of 9/6 jacks or better.

Benefits ★★   User Friendly ★★★   Video Poker ★★★
Casino Rating ★★   Overall Score ★★1/2

Optimal Strategy: Playing loose deuces wild on bonus-point days is best, especially if you enjoy eating and sleeping at the Hacienda. Other than that, I would not go out of my way to play here.

Hard Rock Hotel & Casino
Back Stage Pass (★★)
4475 Paradise Road
(702) 693-5000
(800) 473-7625

Since the Hard Rock Casino opened in early 1995, I've been there a lot. Not because I especially like it, but because it's one of the sights that all my out-of-town visitors want to see. The casino is interesting—open design, constant rock music, custom gaming tables, and lots of memorabilia—but the gambling is mediocre. In other words, if you're a rock fan this is a great place to visit, but if you're looking for value, don't bother with the Hard Rock.

Like many brand new slot clubs, the Back Stage Pass (love that name!) has chosen the way of "don't ask, won't tell." And like other casinos that have taken this path, it doesn't have the personnel to bridge the gap created by the lack of information available to the player. The Hard Rock staff is friendly and extremely hip, but some of them conjure up memories of the opening words to "Star Trek"—"Space, the final frontier..."

The confusing computer system, which is supposed to convey an exact comp-dollar amount, doesn't help much. I once stopped by three separate times over a weekend and asked about my account. Though I hadn't played at all, I got three completely different answers, including "I can't figure this out. Could you play some more and come back later?"

Based on experience, eight hours of dollar play gets you a free room, while two hours of $1 video poker earns a comp for two in the coffee shop. At the Hard Rock, all meal comps are issued in "comp dollars" (scrip in $10 increments), based on the casino's estimate of how much money is needed to cover your meal. I've found these estimates to be high; also, whatever comp dollars you do not spend you lose. My advice is to look at the menu first, do your own (low) estimate, then tell the staff that you'll pay for the difference in cash.

Among the many slot and video poker machines are quarter and dollar 9/6 jacks, 8/5 bonus, and several 8/5 progressives.

Benefits ★   User Friendly ★   Video Poker ★★★
Casino Rating ★★★   Overall Score ★★

Optimal Strategy: For rock revelers only! Check out the 8/5 progressives at the bar, which have been quite high on occasion (the jackpots, not the revelers). Otherwise, stick to 9/6 jacks and enjoy the music.

Harrah's Las Vegas
Gold Card (★★)
3475 Las Vegas Blvd. S.
(702) 369-5000
(800) 427-7247

One of the many riverboats navigating across the Nevada desert, Harrah's Las Vegas was once the largest Holiday Inn in the world. Though many patrons enjoy its upbeat and friendly atmosphere, the food and rooms here are not up to the standards found at other Harrah's properties.

Gold Card members are rewarded with scrip via a secretive system. A supervisor confided that it pays back in scrip approximately 1% on slots and between .33% and .50% on video poker. This disclosure was made only after some serious play and a threat to take my action elsewhere unless I was told how the system worked.

Though I am not fond of scrip and I especially dislike "don't ask, won't tell" systems, Harrah's set-up is more user-friendly then similar set-ups. The scrip can be used throughout the hotel and any unused portions are credited back to your account. Upon checkout, any remaining credits are immediately applied to your hotel bill. The slot booth staff is friendly and I have heard several testimonials regarding cooperative slot hosts.

Harrah's has gaming properties all over America, including Laughlin, Lake Tahoe, Reno, and Atlantic City. Gold Card members from one property receive two free show tickets when they join the club at another property. According to the plan, you'll soon be able to request that scrip earned in any Harrah's casino be credited to your account at any other Harrah's property. I often wonder why other national gaming corporations, such as Circus Circus and Hilton, don't offer a similar deal.

Video poker machine inventory includes quarter and dollar 8/5 bonus and 9/6 progressives. To find them, however, requires a bit of a search.

Benefits ★★★   User Friendly ★★   Video Poker ★★
Casino Rating ★★   Overall Score ★★

Optimal Strategy: This is a good card to carry because of the show-ticket offer, but I wouldn't put serious play on it unless I was planning to use my scrip at one of their other properties.

Imperial Palace Hotel & Casino
Imperial Players Club (★1/2)
3535 Las Vegas Blvd. S.
(702) 794-3158
(800) 351-7400

My feelings toward the Imperial Palace run sweet and sour. This large Oriental-themed maze-like property, heavily booked with tour groups, can be quite confusing, even for the Strip. I enjoy the restaurants, but several visitors I know have complained about the rooms and the out-of-date elevator system (though the men seem to forgive all when they see the cocktail waitress uniforms).

The Imperial Players Club is a recent creation and the entire operation is in the shakedown stage. Granted it's new, but I'll wager that the battle plan was to open the club now and decide how it works later. Offering non-cash rebates only, the club gives you one point for every ten dollars played in any quarter or higher slot or video poker machine. At present, 100 points ($1,000 play) gets you a cheap meal, while 1,000 points ($10,000 play) earns dinner for two at the steakhouse or seafood restaurant. Though the club hints at cash back on some of the literature, it hasn't happened yet and I doubt it ever will.

The club is not particularly user friendly. Players can only check total points after pulling and then re-inserting their card. There is no way to check countdown. There is limited printed material and no newsletter. The booth staff is friendly, but never seems to be sure about what the latest changes are.

With one exception, there is no decent video poker at the Imperial Palace. On the north side of the casino near the tourist information booth are six very old dollar 9/6 progressive jacks, with no max-bet buttons. Playing them requires a great deal of patience.

Benefits ★★   User Friendly ★★   Video Poker ★
Casino Rating ★★   Overall Score ★1/2

Optimal Strategy: Except for the aforementioned dollar 9/6 progressive machines, there is really no reason to play here. The Imperial Palace's rooms and restaurants are only fair, so intangibles are not worth pursuing.

Jerry's Nugget
More Club (★★)
1821 N. Las Vegas Blvd., North Las Vegas
(702) 399-3000
(800) 399-3000

If you love prime rib (not like but love), then Jerry's Nugget is Valhalla. For $8.85 you get 28 ounces of first-prize beef. For $17.70 you die and go to cholesterol heaven with a 56-ounce cut (yeah, that's 3-1/2 pounds). Other than that, with its inconvenient North Las Vegas location, smoky atmosphere, and so-so gambling, I don't find myself here too often.

The More Club offers a cash rebate of .33% on nickels (slots only), .25% on quarters, and .20% for dollars. Forget intangible benefits, or any other assistance beyond the basics. The club's booth, which doubles as a gift shop, is manned sporadically and usually by someone who knows only how to issue vouchers. The club management does not like to answer questions.

Though the card readers reveal your total points, they do not report countdown. I have noted that players with 400 or more points do receive occasional two-for-one meal certificates in the mail.

Machines include quarter 9/6 jacks and 10/7 double bonus, as well as dollar 8/5 bonus jacks. There are no big nickel machines in the joint.

Benefits ★★   User Friendly ★★   Video Poker ★★
Casino Rating ★★   Overall Score ★★

Optimal Strategy: For locals only—an evening of nickel slots or quarter video poker, followed by a big prime rib, can be good cheap fun, especially if done no more than twice a year (remember your health).

Lady Luck Casino & Hotel
Mad Money Club (★★★)
206 North Third Avenue
(702) 477-3000
(800) 525-9582

The Lady Luck, located at the corner of Third and Ogden, successfully combines downtown friendliness and generous gambling with a pinch of Strip glamour.

The Mad Money Club offers cash, scrip, and an extensive VIP program. The club rebates scrip equivalent of 1% slot play and .25% of video poker, based on coin-in, until you earn 10,000 lifetime points ($10,000 in slot action, $40,000 video poker). After that, you begin redeeming points for cash. There are no bonus days, but you can combine table play and slot action for extra comps. Total points and countdown can be checked from any machine.

Intangibles at the Lady Luck are extremely structured via its VIP program. There is no guesswork; the entire program is explained in great detail in a 12-page four-color brochure. Earn 1,000 points a day ($1,000 slot, $4,000 video poker) and you will receive the casino rate. Slot whales who can generate 7,000 points a day get a complimentary suite with fully stocked fridge, all meals in any restaurant, complimentary room service, stretch limo to and from the airport, and use of a private box at the Thomas & Mack Center. (Remember, you get the cash rebates as well.) The Lady Luck is very firm on benefits, so don't try to get more than what's outlined in the brochure.

The Lady Luck has some fine video poker machines, especially if you play jacks or better. Quarter droppers can choose between 8/5 bonus poker or 9/6-4700 jacks; dollar players have 8/5 bonus poker and 9/6-4700 jacks. There are also a couple of 9/6 jacks for big nickel players.

Benefits ★★★   User Friendly ★★★★   Video Poker ★★★
Casino Rating ★★★   Overall Score ★★★

Optimal Strategy: For slot players out there looking for a big comp weekend, this is as good as it gets, especially for only 2-3 hours a day of dollar slot play. Unfortunately, the criterion is a bit high for video poker unless you can play nine hours a day.

Las Vegas Hilton Hotel & Casino
Club Magic (★★1/2)
3000 Paradise Road
(702) 732-5037
(800) 732-7117

Club Magic offers a cash rebate of .5% on all video poker and on $5 slots, 1% on quarter slots, and 1.25% on dollar slots based on a coin-in point system. Though points may be used for scrip in lieu of cash, this is the only slot club in Las Vegas that pays less scrip than cash (150 points earns $15 cash or $10 credit in the restaurants). Any player earning 1,500 points ($15,000 slots, $30,000 video poker) in one day receives total VIP status (for that day), including free rooms and meals in addition to the cash rebate. Club Magic occasionally has double point days, usually in December.

The Las Vegas Hilton features more than 1,150 slot and video poker machines. Unfortunately, fewer than a dozen are truly exciting. These are all quarter machines located near the sports book, including 9/6 jacks, loose deuces wild, and 10/7 double bonus poker. Both quarter and dollar 8/5 bonus and 8/5 jacks progressives are located throughout the casino. In the high-roller area you will find $5 and $25 8/5 bonus and 9/6 jacks. The casino has recently been replacing its full-pay games with less desirable machines, so this situation could change for the worse.

Though some of the machines indicate total points, none of them report the countdown. Most players are forced to check point totals at a large video port. Though booth personnel are affable, they aren't very helpful when asked to supply anything beyond basic information. One nice feature is that vouchers are cashed right at the booth, thus avoiding a trip to the cashier.

Benefits ★★★   User Friendly ★★   Video Poker ★★
Casino Rating ★★★   Overall Score ★★1/2

Optimal Strategy: Restrict your play to the full-pay quarter machines in the sports book, which is an especially pleasant place in the wee hours when the casino runs soft rock videos on nearby big screens. Dollar slot players should check out the RFB program, especially in December if bonus time is offered. Luxury room and board plus a 2.5% cash rebate in exchange for 3 hours of slot play is hard to beat.

Luxor Hotel & Casino
Gold Chamber (★★)
3900 Las Vegas Blvd. S.
(702) 262-4000
(800) 876-0006

My friends love the pyramid. I'm less enthusiastic, though I admit that the architecture, the Nile cruise, King Tut's Museum, and diagonal elevators are intriguing. "The Search for the Obelisk" attractions on the second floor provide a lot of thrills for a good price. Maybe it's because the casino's low ceilings make me feel like I'm gambling in a basement (or a subterranean burial chamber).

The Gold Chamber operates on the identical formula used in other Circus Circus properties. You get a cash rebate of .25%, but only after acquiring 400 points ($4,000 coin-in), making you a permanent member. All permanent members receive a 50% discount on rooms. Be aware that Luxor rooms and meals can be priced considerably higher than those at Excalibur or Circus Circus.

Players can check points and countdown from any machine. The countdown is not retained so don't pull your card too early. The Gold Chamber booth personnel are especially helpful. Extra comped meals can be obtained through the slot host after $3,000-$4,000 play.

Among the limited video poker selection, you'll find (if you search) a few quarter 8/5 bonus, 8/5 progressive, 8/5 bonus progressive, and 10/7 double bonus. There are no worthwhile dollar video poker machines to speak of. The Luxor has nickel 10/7 double bonus, but these do not qualify for slot club points.

Benefits ★★   User Friendly ★★★   Video Poker ★
Casino Rating ★★★   Overall Score ★★

Optimal Strategy: If you like Luxor, join the club and run up 400 points. You'll get $10 cash, and 50% off the rack rate for a room for at least eighteen months. These are, after all, the only hotel rooms in town with slanted walls.

MGM Grand Hotel, Casino and Theme Park
MGM Players Club (★★)
3799 Las Vegas Blvd. S.
(702) 891-3651
(800) 929-9410

Hollywood, the Emerald City, Monte Carlo, and Disneyland notwithstanding, the MGM Grand still has little to offer the quarter and dollar player. Slot whales (high rollers), however, may find a good home at the MGM.

Player's Club cash rebates are based on coin-in. The system is tiered, and players who accrue more points receive a higher cashrebate return. Slot and video poker players receive a .125% rebate for $200 worth of action, .25% for $20,000, .375% for $60,000, .5% for $200,000, .75% for $400,000 and .88% for $800,000 of play. That's a lot of quarters (or even dollars) just to get what amounts to an average rebate.

You receive a permanent card when you earn 2,000 points ($200 action), but in reality, the club doesn't treat you as a fully activated member until you reach 20,000 ($2,000 worth of action), which entitles you to the casino rate and other perks.

Despite the multitude of slot and video poker machines, there are no quarter or dollar full-pay deuces, 9/6 jacks, or even 10/7 double bonus. Until recently the MGM did offer $5 9/6 jacks in its high limit slot area, but those have been replaced by lower paying machines. At press time the casino has 8/5 bonus and 8/6 jacks progressives, as well as $25 and $100 9/6 machines.

The Player's Club booth is open 24 hours a day to issue cash vouchers. Unfortunately, I find the staff to be somewhat abrupt. Slot hosts are hard to find and the booth personnel always have an excuse not to issue a meal comp. Though a player can check points at any slot machine, the system frequently gets overloaded on busy weekends, causing a several-hour delay in processing point totals. This club, like the casino in general, has a ways to go.

Benefits ★   User Friendly ★★   Video Poker ★
Casino Rating ★★★★   Overall Score ★★

Optimal Strategy: If (in your mind) there just couldn't be a better place to stay than the MGM Grand, then run $2,000 through a machine and get the 50% casino rate discount.

Mirage Hotel & Casino
Club Mirage (★★★)
3400 Las Vegas Blvd. S.
(702) 791-7111
(800) 627-5687

When The Mirage opened on Thanksgiving 1989, it was the most important event on the Las Vegas Strip since Bugsy opened the Flamingo. The Mirage set the megaresort standard, and though others have opened bigger, not one has opened better.

Club Mirage is a direct import from the downtown Golden Nugget 24 Karat Club, with a few changes. The club gives a cash rebate of .67% for dollar and up play, as well as additional room and meal comps. There is no difference in rebates and rewards between video poker and slots. There are two booths, both competently staffed, where you can go for cash rebates and other extras such as line passes. Though the booth handles additional intangible comps, the slot hosts can be more flexible than the booth personnel.

New members are granted temporary membership until they accumulate 150 points ($2,250 in action). Upon graduation you receive $15 in cash and two free buffets. Full membership also includes unlimited line passes (which are a blessing when trying to eat at the popular Mirage buffet on weekends). Members who accumulate an additional 50 points per day ($750 in action) while staying at the hotel are granted the casino rate. Mirage properties have very user-friendly slot clubs, though they never have bonus days and handle table-play comps under a separate system.

Unfortunately, the only dollar machines close to decent at The Mirage are 8/5 bonus poker. Five-dollar whales can choose between 8/5 bonus and 9/6 jacks, including two progressives. Note: Though quarter play is not included in Club Mirage, you can find quarter 9/6 jacks throughout the casino.

Benefits ★★★★   User Friendly ★★★★   Video Poker ★
Casino Rating ★★★★   Overall Score ★★★

Optimal Strategy: If you play dollar slots or video poker, The Mirage should be one of your first stops. For $2,250 in action (on 8/5 bonus machines, that's a theoretical loss of $20), you get $15 in cash, two free buffets, the casino rate, and VIP treatment at the Strip's most glamorous megaresort. After that, you can move your dollar video poker action next door to Caesars Palace (they have 9/6 jacks) and still impress your friends—"I never stand in line to eat at The Mirage."

Nevada Palace Hotel & Casino
Player's Circle (★1/2)
5255 Boulder Highway
(702) 458-8810
(800) 634-6283

The Nevada Palace, just south of Sam's Town, is one of the most uncooperative casinos I have ever encountered. Whenever I ask a question, I get an earful of "who wants to know." I'm lucky. Bob Dancer was followed by several rather large security guards as he was surveying the video poker machines. If all this makes ya' wonder how they treat big winners, two other players of my acquaintance have commented on the unusual length of time the casino takes to pay off a jackpot.

For what it's worth, the Player's Circle pays a .125% cash rebate on slots and video poker. Double and triple bonus times are common. On your birthday you receive a coupon worth 500 points that can be redeemed for $1.25 and a free T-shirt. According to the slot club staff, they occasionally comp a meal to either of the two restaurants located in the casino. The eateries are mediocre at best.

Among the video poker machines, you will find quarter and dollar 8/5 bonus.

Benefits ★★   User Friendly ★   Video Poker ★★
Casino Rating ★   Overall Score ★1/2

Optimal Strategy: Sign up, wait for your birthday, and see if you get the coupon for $1.25 and a T-shirt.

Palace Station Hotel & Casino
buy-in log system (not rated)
2411 W. Sahara Ave.
(702) 367-2411
(800) 544-2411

Probably the most popular "locals" casino in Las Vegas, Palace Station first opened (under the name Bingo Palace) as a spot where Strip workers went to gamble after-shift. In the past 15 years, both the casino and its parent company, Station Casinos, have grown tremendously.

The casino's main attraction is its restaurants, from The Feast, its excellent buffet, to the more upscale Pasta Palace and Fisherman's Broiler. Food comps are the number-one reason to play here.

Station Casinos has announced that in November 1995, it will completely abandon the buy-in log-book method of rating and comping players. In its place will be a computerized tracking system, known as the Boarding Pass, similar to the club at the newest Station property, Texas. According to various casino sources, the three casinos' systems will eventually be blended into one, so players can earn comps at one casino and spend them at another.

I will reserve judgment until the Boarding Pass system is completely operational. Station Casinos is competing in the tough local market, so one can expect some early fits and starts.

At Palace Station, video poker machine inventory changes often as management is quick to remove an unprofitable machine. For now, the best of the lot are several quarter and dollar 8/5 bonus poker sequentials, 10/7 double bonus, and 9/6 double bonus sequential progressives.

Optimal Strategy: Palace Station is worth a stop to enjoy the good food and service. Once the Boarding Pass system is up and running, stop by, join the club, play for an hour or so, and see what develops.

Rio Suite Hotel and Casino
Play Rio (★★★)
3700 West Flamingo Road
(702) 252-7717
(800) 752-9746

The Rio does well in the annual *Las Vegas Review-Journal* reader poll, and in this case I agree with the voters. The Rio has the best buffet and the sexiest cocktail waitresses in town. This is also Las Vegas' only all-suite hotel-casino, and while the suites do not match the high-roller haunts at The Mirage, they are very classy.

For many years the Rio worked on a buy-in system. It was easy to exploit and many did. About a year ago the Rio computerized and now bases all comps on a time system. For example, three to five hours play on a 25¢ slot or video poker machine is worth a free buffet, while three to five hours of $1 play gets dinner at Antonio's Italian restaurant. Though these comps are technically for one person, you can sometimes get them for two with no additional play, especially if you go through a slot host. More than at any other Las Vegas property, I strongly recommend that you find a slot host to negotiate comps at the Rio. If you have to go to the booth, ask to see a host. One is usually stationed nearby.

Because of past abuses, the current system is not user-friendly. The card readers tell you nothing except that your play is being credited. On my last visit, there were no brochures and the booth staff would not answer any specific questions without the permission of a supervisor.

Quarter players can choose among 9/6-4700 jacks, 8/5 bonus poker with Sneaky Rita (an extra bonus payoff), full-pay deuces, 10/7 double bonus, and 9/6 jacks with 2nd Chance progressive (which is frequently worth more than 101%); dollar players are looking at 8/5 bonus sequential progressive, 9/6 jacks, and 9/6 jacks with 2nd Chance progressive.

Benefits ★★   User Friendly ★★   Video Poker ★★★★
Casino Rating ★★★★   Overall Score ★★★

Optimal Strategy: The line to get into the Rio's Carnival World Buffet is the longest in Las Vegas. To avoid it, go to the booth (or ask a host) for a "dollar-off" buffet coupon, which also serves as a VIP line pass for two people. Though this requires about 15 minutes of quarter slot play, it could save more than an hour in wait time. (Although not officially sanctioned, just showing your Play Rio card to the cashier can sometimes qualify you for the VIP line.)

Riviera Hotel & Casino
Gold Club (★★1/2)
2901 Las Vegas Blvd. S.
(702) 734-5110
(800) 634-3420

When built in 1955, the nine-story Riviera was the tallest structure on the Strip. Since then, the casino has expanded umpteen times to become one of the largest casinos in the United States with over 125,000 square feet of gaming space. The Riv's forty-year journey has not been without some financial ups and downs; the casino recently worked its way out of Chapter 11.

Don't let any of this deter you from playing here, as the Riviera has one of the better slot clubs in the neighborhood, with a cash rebate of 1% for slot play and .5% for video poker. If, in lieu of cash, you ask for "Riviera Bucks," which can be used anywhere in the hotel, or a buffet comp your rewards can be worth an additional 10%-50%. (Be aware that the food is not among the town's best.)

Members with more than 200 lifetime points ($1,000 slots, $2,000 video poker) are entitled to the casino rate for the next two years. Depending on the day of the week, this could be as low as $19 and as high as $49. Long-term members frequently receive free-room offers in the mail.

Though the countdown resets upon card removal, this is one of the few clubs in town that warns players about it in the literature. Both total points and countdown can be checked at all machines and cards should be shown when playing at the tables.

Unfortunately, the large Gold Club booth is poorly located in the rear of the maze-like casino. The staff could be a bit more helpful. Many members mistakenly attempt to redeem points at the much more prominent Gambler's Spree booth and are curtly directed to the other booth.

The Riv's machine selection includes quarter 8/5 bonus and 9/6 jacks. Dollar players will find 8/5 bonus, 9/6 jacks, 8/5 progressives, and 9/6 double bonus with triple progressives.

Benefits ★★★   User Friendly ★★   Video Poker ★★★
Casino Rating ★★   Overall Score ★★1/2

Optimal Strategy: Good cash rebates and satisfactory video poker make the Riviera a decent choice for the Strip. Earn at least 200 points to get the casino rate and an occasional comp. Unless you're a hotel guest or like the Riv's buffet, redeem your points for cash.

Sahara Hotel and Casino
Preferred Gold Card (★★★)
2535 Las Vegas Blvd. S.
(702) 737-2111
(800) 634-6411

Once the undisputed queen of the north Strip, the antiquated Sahara lacks the excitement and glamour of the younger resorts. But if you're after full-pay (or better) video poker combined with strong promotions and easy-to-obtain comps, the Sahara becomes worthy of serious consideration.

Preferred Gold Card members do not receive cash. They get free rooms and meals via a buy-in system. After signing up for the club, you're assigned a number and given a laminated card. Then the casino keeps track of how many coins you purchase via punch cards obtained from the cashier. Every time you buy additional coins or insert money into the currency receptor on a machine, have one of the change personnel punch in the appropriate amount. (Hint: Remember not to keep playing the same money over and over again.) When the punch card has the amount needed to obtain a desired comp (see below), turn it in to the booth and make your request. When playing blackjack or any other table game, show your laminated card to the floorman.

For a buy-in (or accrued buy-ins) of $200, the club will treat you to a buffet for one. (Please note that the Sahara buffet is not among the best in town.) A $450 buy-in is good for a coffee shop comp for two. If you want to shoot for one of the more expensive restaurants, combine at least a $1,000 buy-in with some polite negotiation.

Video poker reigns supreme at the Sahara. Standouts included quarter 9/6-4795 jacks, full-pay deuces, and one four-coin 9/6-4000 jacks machine. Standard five-coin 9/6 jacks are offered at the dollar and $5 levels.

Note: In June 1995, the Sahara was sold to William Bennett, former CEO of Circus Circus. Any and all of the above may be changed in the near future.

Benefits ★★★   User Friendly ★★★   Video Poker ★★★★
Casino Rating ★★   Overall Score ★★★

Optimal Strategy: Buy $450 worth of quarters, and play one of the better machines mentioned above. Afterwards, treat a friend to a nice meal in the coffee shop. The Sahara is another source for good cheap rooms.

Sam's Town Hotel & Gambling Hall
Town Club (★★★1/2)
5111 Boulder Highway
(702) 456-7777
(800) 897-8696

According to local legend, Sam Boyd built his popular casino at Boulder Highway and Nellis Blvd., exactly halfway between the California in downtown Las Vegas and the Eldorado in Henderson. This allowed him to stop and get a drink between properties. Whatever his reason, Sam's Town quickly became a hit, particularly with the hard-to-please local crowd, and is a principal player on the Boulder strip. A much needed expansion completed in July 1994 added 450 hotel rooms, a nine-story atrium, and a dancing-waters laser show. A bowling alley, dance hall, well-stocked country western store, and a child-care center are also available.

The Town Club returns a paltry .09% cash rebate based on a coin-in point system. All slot and video poker machines are included (good news for little nickel players). Occasionally Sam's offers double points. In June 1995, slot and pit promotions were combined; now slot club cards can be used for table-play ratings.

Sam's Town is an excellent example of why you shouldn't judge slot clubs by cash rebate alone. The casino is generous with intangibles. For example, $2,500 of play usually gets you a dinner for two at Papamio's, the Italian restaurant, while about $3,500 in play earns a similar comp at Billy Bob's, the new steakhouse (there are eight excellent restaurants at Sam's Town). Remember to speak to a slot host and not the Town Club booth personnel to arrange dinner comps.

Machine selection is very good, particularly at the quarter level. Besides 9/6 jacks progressives and 10/7 double bonus, Sam's Town features an unique deuces game called bonus deuces. With perfect play, you can achieve a 100.9% return, and that's before you figure in slot club benefits. Dollar players will find 8/5 progressive bonus jacks, 10/7 double bonus, and one 9/6 jacks in the high-roller area.

Benefits ★★★   User Friendly ★★★★   Video Poker ★★★★
Casino Rating ★★★   Overall Score ★★★1/2

Optimal Strategy: Play between $2,500 and $3,500, find a slot host, and work the intangibles. If you play more than 100 hours a year, buy a computer program and take the time to learn bonus deuces, an excellent opportunity to beat the house. Also, be on the lookout for seasonal promos.

Sands Hotel & Casino
Sandsational Slot Club (★★)
3355 Las Vegas Blvd. S.
(702) 733-5000
(800) 446-4678

Thirty years ago, the Sands was the playground of the "Rat Pack": Frank Sinatra, Sammy Davis Jr., Peter Lawford, Joey Bishop, Dean Martin, and various friends. In the midst of the megaresorts, the Sands evokes a nostalgia for the '50s. Though the casino has been expanded and upgraded, the rest of the hotel hasn't. Thus you get an interesting combination of modern gambling with old-fashioned lodging.

The Sandsational Slot Club rebates .33% based on coin-out with weekly double-point days. To become a full member you must earn 50 points ($750 coins returned). The club's brochure states that other intangible benefits, such as discounted and free rooms, comped meals, special invitations, are based on coin-in. I recently received an offer in the mail for a meal comp for two at the Xanadu steakhouse. A nice surprise.

Of late, the Sands has been attempting to promote and simplify its club. The booth has been relocated to the front of the casino. Unlike other coin-out systems, both countdown and total points can be checked at any machine.

Video poker selection at the Sands is abysmal. The only machines worth checking are the 8/5 bonus or the 8/5 jacks progressives if the jackpot is higher than $2,200.

Benefits ★★   User Friendly ★★★   Video Poker ★
Casino Rating ★★   Overall Score ★★

Optimal Strategy: Play the 8/5 bonus or 8/5 jacks progressives during double-bonus days. Earn 50 points, go for a comp, and get your name on the mailing list for possible offers.

San Remo Las Vegas Casino & Resort
Money Club (★★★1/2)
115 East Tropicana Ave.
(702) 739-9000
(800) 522-7366

This casino deserves a lot more attention that it gets. Quietly located just east of the crowded Tropicana-Las Vegas Blvd. intersection, the San Remo affords players a better slot club return than most of its well-known neighbors.

The Money Club pays above-average cash rebates, especially for high-end slot players. Dollar and $5 slot action gets a .83% cash rebate, quarter players earn .50%, and nickel players (remember them?) get a .24% rebate. Video poker players don't do quite as well. Dollar and $5 play earns .33%, quarter players get .14%, and nickel players a .17% cash rebate return.

Recently the San Remo instituted a special "Double Dining" promotion. Players earning at least 500 points in three days get matching points if redeemed for restaurant meals. Qualifying requires about $1,000 in quarter slot play, $3,000 in quarter video poker play, or $1,500 action played through a dollar video poker machine.

Points and countdown (which reset upon card removal) can be checked at any machine or by asking the friendly slot booth staff.

The Money Club offers complimentary rooms and meals above and beyond the tangibles (including Double Dining) and they're up front about what's required and what's delivered by way of a well-written four-color brochure. For example, two hours of dollar slot play or four hours of dollar video poker gets dinner for two at the Ristorante Del Fiori coffee shop.

Best of all, the San Remo has some decent video poker machines, including quarter full-pay deuces, 8/5 bonus jacks, and 9/6 jacks, as well as dollar and $5 9/6 jacks. Effectively combining the better machines with the Money Club produces one of the best deals on the south Strip.

Benefits ★★★   User Friendly ★★★★   Video Poker ★★★★
Casino Rating ★★★   Overall Score ★★★1/2

Optimal Strategy: If you're near the south Strip, check out the San Remo. Besides good video poker and above-average cash rebates, an hour's worth of dollar action or four hours of quarters will get a decent meal comp. You won't find a better combination at any of the nearby properties.

Santa Fe Hotel & Casino
Player's Edge (★★★)
4949 North Rancho Drive
(702) 658-4900
(800) 872-6823

The Santa Fe is the first casino that visitors encounter when driving in from the northwest and the last of the Lowden family's Las Vegas casinos (former owners of the Sahara and Hacienda).

Like the Sahara, the Santa Fe awards comps based on buy-in. Every time you buy coins or insert currency into a machine, ask the change person to punch the amount on a Player's Edge punch card. Put the money through the machine at least once. Before you leave the casino, write your name and ID number on the punch card and turn it in at the Player's Edge desk. If you want your comp immediately, say so before surrendering your card, otherwise just come by the next day and they'll check your account on the computer. Once you get the hang of the system, you'll find that it's easy to use.

A $100 buy-in often gets a buffet comp, $250 an unlimited coffee shop meal. Frankly the food at the Santa Fe is so-so and the service is snail-paced. They've added several new restaurants recently (gourmet, steakhouse, Italian, and the only Ben & Jerry's outlet in Las Vegas), which I've heard good things about.

The Player's Edge Club offers excellent benefits just for joining (no play required). Members receive substantial discounts on bowling and ice skating, and on weekdays can get 2-for-1 buffet meals. The club's colorful newsletter has an easy-to-read calendar that details upcoming promotions.

Machines include quarter full-pay deuces and 9/6 jacks progressives. Dollar players will find both 9/6 jacks and 9/6 jacks progressives (the latter are available at the bar).

Note: Several Santa Fe employees inform me that the current system is on its last legs and will be replaced by some form of computerized tracking system.

Benefits ★★★   User Friendly ★★★   Video Poker ★★★★
Casino Rating ★★   Overall Score ★★★

Optimal Strategy: Make a large buy-in. Put the money through once and turn it in for currency at the cashier. If you want to continue playing, buy in again. Don't forget to get the buy-ins logged. Then turn your card in for a comp.

Showboat Hotel & Casino
Officer's Club (★★1/2)
2800 Fremont Street
(702) 385-9123
(800) 826-2800

For many years, the Showboat Hotel has scored high marks in the annual *Las Vegas Review-Journal* Best of Las Vegas poll. While hushed accusations of "stuffing the ballot box" have been leveled, the operation is friendly and low key, and successfully maintains a strong local following. Recently, business has been negatively impacted by the new Boulder Station and the much-improved Sam's Town.

The casino is currently immersed in a renovation project of its own, which won't be completed until spring '96. Until that time, slot club policies seem to be in a state of flux. For example, the Officer's Club officially pays a cash rebate of .25% for slots and .125% for video poker, but during the casino construction phase, these rebates have been doubled. The club has discontinued both its brochure and newsletter until spring '96.

The Officer's Club is tiered: Pilot, Admiral, Top Gun, etc. Because of construction status, written material explaining the advantages of each level is not available, though I was told by the staff that bonus points are earned upon graduation to each rank.

Machine selection at the Showboat is decent, particularly for jacks or better players. Quarter players can choose from 8/5 bonus, 9/6 jacks, or 10/7 double bonus. Fifty-cent and dollar players have all of the above, plus several 9/6-4500 machines. Players can check total points and countdown at any machine and the slot club staff is extremely helpful.

Benefits ★★   User Friendly ★★★   Video Poker ★★★
Casino Rating ★★   Overall Score ★★1/2

Optimal Strategy: I'll wait to see the new Showboat before rendering a final opinion. At present, 50¢ and $1 players can do well playing 9/6-4500 jacks combined with the .25% rebate.

Stardust Hotel & Casino
Stardust Slot Club (★★1/2)
3000 Las Vegas Blvd. S.
(702) 732-6111
(800) 634-6757

The Stardust's fascinating history began in 1955 when Anthony Cornero dreamed of building the biggest and most lavish hotel in the world. (Where have we heard that before, or since?) Between Cornero's sudden death at a Desert Inn crap table in 1958 and the Stardust's 1985 acquisition by the Boyd Group, the hotel had a series of owners who knew the fifth amendment better than my civics professor.

The Stardust Slot Club pays a cash rebate of .33% for quarter slots, .40% for quarter and half-dollar video poker, and .50% on all dollar action based on coin-in. The club frequently designates an entire month as double-point month. Members can also receive additional room and meal comps in an amount equal to their cash rebate.

Both the casino and the slot club treat their long-term customers well. Get in the database and give them some play to get offers in the mail for free hotel nights.

Total points and countdown can be checked at all machines, and the club's written materials are very helpful. Though the slot club booth is well located and well-staffed, many people mistake it for the casino cashier, so frequently half the line is in the wrong place.

At the Stardust the countdown is retained by the machine, not the card. You can make a rather profitable game of finding a machine with a low countdown, earning the point, then moving on to the next lowest countdown. It can be a bit time-consuming, though.

Among the best machines are quarter 8/5 bonus, 8/5 triple progressives (increasing jackpots for four-of-a-kind, straight flush, and royal flush), 10/7 double bonus (hidden in the Game Maker), and half-dollar 9/6 jacks. Dollar 9/6 machines can be found at the bar in the keno lounge.

Benefits ★★★   User Friendly ★★★   Video Poker ★★
Casino Rating ★★★   Overall Score ★★1/2

Optimal Strategy: This is one of the better clubs for earning free and almost-free rooms once you're known. Seek out the half-dollar 9/6 games, especially during double-point months.

Texas Gambling Hall & Hotel
Player's Club (★★)
2101 Texas Star Lane, North Las Vegas
(702) 631-1000
(800) 654-8888

When is a slot club not a slot club? When it's deep in the heart of Texas! The staff at the newest Station Casino property located on Rancho Drive in North Las Vegas will correct you if you refer to their "tracking system" as a "slot club." Only a few years ago, Palace Station, Station's first casino, ran a still-famous "no slot club" advertising campaign.

Whatever they call it, what you get is a "don't ask, won't tell" secretive system. Though the card can be used anywhere in the casino (including the tables and in the sports book), there is no way for a player to determine what comps are coming to him. According to the staff, comps are based on what you play, how long you play, and how much you win or lose. By November 1995, identical systems will be operating at both Palace and Boulder Stations.

The casino itself is quite amusing. The decor features a big mirrored armadillo in the Armadillo Honky Tonk, as well as custom carpeting covered with Texas graphics throughout. Also, check out the Texas-shaped bricks on the aprons just outside the doorways.

As always, players can get better and more frequent comps by befriending a slot host. To its credit, Texas has a lot of them. After an hour of $1 video poker, contact a slot host and ask for a dinner comp to the excellent Stockyard Steakhouse. If you don't get it on the spot, you will after a small amount of additional play. An hour of quarter play should get you two comped dinners at the so-so buffet.

Video poker selection includes an abundance of quarter and dollar 9/6 jacks and 10/7 double bonus, as well as several other variations you will not find anywhere else. Though Station Casinos have a habit of removing machines with good schedules, competition from the neighboring Fiesta may dictate otherwise.

Benefits ★★   User Friendly ★   Video Poker ★★★
Casino Rating ★★★   Overall Score ★★

Optimal Strategy: If you live in or frequent northwest Las Vegas, then give Texas a try. Sign up for the slot club (oops, sorry, the player tracking system), play either 9/6 jacks or 10/7 double bonus for an hour, then try to hook up with an agreeable slot host.

Tom's Sunset Casino
Slot Seeker's Club (★★1/2)
444 W. Sunset Road, Henderson
(702) 564-5551

This is southern Nevada's smallest slot club. Located in Henderson just southeast of Las Vegas, between Boulder Highway and the Green Valley residential area, Tom's has 240 slot machines, along with a half-dozen table games. There is a small restaurant and lounge, but no hotel rooms.

The Slot Seeker's Club pays .25% for video poker and slots based on a coin-out system. On Mondays, Tuesdays, and Wednesdays, the club features double-bonus time; it occasionally offers additional bonuses during the wee hours. Though you must earn an initial 6,000 points (approximately $6,000 in action) to receive cash vouchers, all members are put on the mailing list for a monthly newsletter filled with discount meal coupons and special offers.

Machine selection at Tom's is limited but decent. At the quarter level, you will find full-pay deuces, 10/7 double bonus, 8/5 bonus jacks, and 8/5 progressives. The only good dollar machines are a smattering of 8/5 bonus jacks. You can check point levels at every machine. The booth personnel, as well as casino management, are extremely friendly and helpful.

Benefits ★★   User Friendly ★★★★   Video Poker ★★★
Casino Rating ★   Overall Score ★★1/2

Optimal Strategy: Locals should make the trip to Henderson just to sign up and get on the newsletter list. Restrict your play to the full-pay quarter machines Monday through Wednesday.

Treasure Island Hotel & Casino
Treasure Island Club (★★★)
3300 Las Vegas Blvd. S.
(702) 894-7111
(800) 944-3777

Treasure Island gets the details right, from the skulls on the entrance doors to the chandeliers made of "bones." The outdoor pirate fight, staged gratis several times each night, is the hottest show—literally—in town.

The Treasure Island Slot Club has almost identical policies and features as Club Mirage next door. Only dollar machines and up qualify for slot club points. Cash rebates are .67% of total play, either slot or video poker. To receive a permanent card and your first $15 rebate voucher, you must play through $2,250 in action. As a permanent member you are automatically entitled to the casino rate, line-pass privileges, and other forms of VIP treatment. To maintain your casino-rate status, you should play through at least $750 per day on subsequent trips.

In addition to cash rebates, Treasure Island gives out food and room comps worth another .67%. Though the whole process is handled very efficiently at the booth, I still recommend going though slot hosts, who are more apt to bend the rules a bit.

Similar to the clubs at all Steve Wynn properties, the Treasure Island slot club is extremely user-friendly. You can check point totals at any machine. The countdown is not lost if you change machines. The staff in the booth is first class. The club does not have a newsletter, but you can expect to receive some nice complimentaries in the mail, especially on your birthday.

Just before this book went to press, Treasure Island removed its few dollar 9/6 jacks. There are still big nickel and up 9/6 jacks and a few dollar 8/5 bonus jacks.

Benefits ★★★★   User Friendly ★★★★   Video Poker ★
Casino Rating ★★★★   Overall Score ★★★

Optimal Strategy: Dollar players and up only. Get a temporary card, then find an 8/5 bonus machine. After you earn 150-200 points ($2,250-$3,000 play), go to the booth for your $15 cash rebate and two buffets. While you're there, introduce yourself to a slot host for future comps.

Tropicana Resort and Casino
Island Winner's Club (★★)
3801 Las Vegas Blvd. S.
(702) 739-2711
(800) 521-8767

The Island Winner's Club is the original secretive system. When you insert your card into one of the Trop's card readers, all it says is "Card Accepted." When you ask the staff how much play is required to earn cash and comps, they say, "It's different for every machine in the house, so we cannot answer that question."

Based on conversations with Tropicana executives and a study done several years back by the *Las Vegas Advisor*, it appears that the Island Winner's Club returns 14% of the house's theoretical win on all dollar machines and 8% on quarters. The disbursements are made two-thirds in cash, one-third in comps. Under that assumption, if you play a five-coin dollar video poker machine with a theoretical house win of 3% at a rate of 600 pulls an hour for two hours, you get a cash rebate of $16 and comps worth $8. This example computes to an acceptable .4% total rebate based on coin-in, but under this formula, the rebate percentage decreases rapidly if you choose a machine with a lower house edge, such as 9/6 jacks.

Though the card may be used at the tables, cash rebates are only given for slot and video poker play. Comps are given in scrip that can be used at any restaurant or gift shop in the hotel, or applied to your room. Though the benefit schedule is not great, the Tropicana does offer a good innovative deal for new members. Play any slot or video poker machine or any table game for three hours and you get a free room. (You have to pay the rack rate for any additional nights.) The casino stocks quarter full-pay deuces and 9/6 jacks, as well as dollar 9/6 jacks, so this can be an excellent deal. It also puts you on the mailing list for possible future offers.

Benefits ★★   User Friendly ★   Video Poker ★★★
Casino Rating ★★★   Overall Score ★★

Optimal Strategy: New members should play three hours on a good quarter machine and get a free room for one night. If you really like the hotel, stick to the full-pay deuces or 9/6 jacks.

Westward Ho Casino
Preferred Customer Card (★★1/2)
2900 Las Vegas Blvd. S.
(702) 731-2900
(800) 223-1709

The Westward Ho is one of the least expensive resorts on the Strip. It also has a reputation for being one of the friendliest. During a recent visit, I was treated to a short history (over the public address system) of craps and blackjack.

The Preferred Customer Card pays a small cash rebate for slots: .20% for dollars, .29% for quarters, and .47% for nickels. For video poker they pay .07% for dollars and quarters and .16% for nickels.

The major benefit is rooms. Though the hotel will not give details, I've heard that the casino rate of $19.20 (even on New Year's Eve) can be obtained with only a couple of hours of quarter play, or several more hours of nickels (about 1,000 points). The accommodations are far from plush (though it may be the best place in town for very large "low-roller suites"), the place is safe, clean, and centrally located on the Strip.

Members who've earned 1,000 points also receive (with no points deducted) two free tickets to one of the casinos special events, such as a luau or barbecue. These offers may include complimentary rooms, depending on your individual level of play.

This is not an easy club to use. The readout displays are the smallest in town, and do not report total points or countdown. Though the club has a four-color brochure, explanations are confusing. There is no printed prize list. Both the list and a point-information terminal can be found around the corner from the booth.

Among the better machines are quarter 9/6 progressives, full-pay deuces, and 9/6 jacks, dollar 9/6 jacks, and for nickel players 8/5 progressives.

Benefits ★★★   User Friendly ★★   Video Poker ★★★★
Casino Rating ★   Overall Score ★★1/2

Optimal Strategy: If you play nickel slots and want to stay on the Strip, then the Westward Ho is your spot. Run up 1,000 points (it'll take about 5 hours on a five-coin nickel machine) and you'll become a member of the family.

9

Beyond Las Vegas

The current outbreak of slot club fever in southern Nevada is not restricted to Las Vegas. It has reached other gambling destinations in the region, including Jean, Mesquite, and Laughlin.

Slot clubs seem to run in packs. I have yet to see a region with just one; when one casino starts a slot club, many others follow suit. For example, until recently there were no slot clubs at either of the Mesquite casinos. Then Merv Griffin opened the Player's Island Casino, complete with slot club. Overnight the nearby Virgin River added a club as well.

Because I was able to check each of the non-Las Vegas casinos only a few times, I cannot write a comprehensive review of each. I've supplied basic information and recommended my favorites.

JEAN

Jean is located between Las Vegas and the California border. It has five casinos, including those at the state line eight miles west. The three Primm family properties at the state line (Whiskey Pete's, Primadonna's, and Buffalo Bill's) do not have slot clubs at this time.

Gold Strike Casino - Strike It Rich Club
Nevada Landing - Lucky Landing Club

These properties are almost identical. I'm particularly fond of Nevada Landing with its riverboat exterior, beamed ceilings, and massive chandeliers. Both casinos were recently purchased by Circus Circus. Though both slot clubs pay a small .10% cash rebate, they're generous with meal comps. Except for a few 9/6 jacks, neither has great video poker.

The state line casinos have the big attractions (including the world's tallest roller coaster), but you can save a few bucks on food and lodging by using slot club benefits at either of these hotels.

LAUGHLIN

In 1966, Don Laughlin took over an eight-room motel on the Colorado River and the rest is history. There are ten casinos on the Laughlin strip, nine of which have slot clubs. February 1995 saw the opening of the first Indian casino in southern Nevada on the nearby Mojave Indian Reservation.

Laughlin, with its inexpensive accommodations and friendly service, seems to bring out the party in everyone. The last time I took my father and stepmother there, they stayed up until 2 a.m. every night playing slots, video poker, and even flip-it. When I reminded them on our final night in Laughlin that we had to drive back to Las Vegas the next morning, they told me, "You'll have to drive so we can sleep in the car."

Though slot club cash rebates are lower in Laughlin than Las Vegas, almost every casino regularly schedules double-point bonus days. The casinos are generous with additional rooms and meals. On my first trip I took my own advice and signed up for every club. Within two months I'd received a free-room offer from almost every casino.

Laughlin slot clubs are user friendly. Unless noted otherwise, all systems give the total points and countdown. Almost all the clubs have extensive written materials (including newsletters) and well-staffed booths.

Warning: Laughlin is always about eight degrees warmer than Las Vegas. In July 1994, the temperature reached a Nevada record of 125 degrees. Low humidity or not, that's hot!

Avi Hotel & Casino - Advantage Club

Located 10 miles south of Laughlin, the Avi is owned and operated by the Mojave Indians. The club rebates .49% in cash. On my last visit, after playing a $1 machine for an hour, several staff members separately offered to comp lunch. The best machines are quarter and dollar 8/5 jacks progressives. The system tells you total points, but not the countdown.

Colorado Belle Hotel & Casino - Club Belle
Edgewater Hotel & Casino - Winner's Edge

These side-by-side properties are both operated by Circus Circus. Club rebates (.25%) and machines (8/5 bonus poker and 8/5 jacks progressives) are identical at both properties. The clubs occasionally run bonus promotions (double-triple-quadruple). In addition to the rebates, both clubs comp meals to members.

Don Laughlin's Riverside - King of Slot Clubs

The original resort is still one of the nicest (though it has grown from eight rooms to 1,404 and is a bit of a maze). The King of Clubs pays a straightforward .20% cash rebate on both slots and video poker. You can earn your points on either quarter or dollar 9/6 jacks or 8/5 bonus machines. Monday is frequently double-point day.

Flamingo Hilton Laughlin - Magic Club

This casino looks the most "Las Vegas" of all the properties in Laughlin. The Magic Club pays a .32% rebate for slots and .16% for video poker, with frequent double-point times. If you'd prefer a meal or logoed items in lieu of cash, points are worth twice as much. 9/6 jacks can be found at all denominations. Be aware that the point system is set up so that all machines have countdowns of 25.

Gold River Hotel & Gambling Hall - Gaming Society

This property has gone through several management changes in recent years and has yet to hit its stride. Management is revamping the current secretive system into something resembling the systems found at the Circus Circus properties. The hotel has several 9/6 jacks at both the quarter and dollar levels.

Golden Nugget - 24 Karat Club

Depending on what you play (slots, video poker) and how you play it (quarters, dollars), the 24 Karat Club rebates .11%-.67%. There's a nice selection of machines, including quarter full-pay deuces, 10/7 double bonus, and 9/6-4700 jacks, as well as dollar 8/5 bonus and 9/6 jacks. They do not offer bonus times, but every month or so I receive a free weekday room offer in the mail.

Harrah's Casino Hotel - Gold Card

This is one classy place for one low price. Situated on a hill on the south end of town, many of the elegantly furnished rooms have a superb view of the Laughlin strip and the Colorado River. The club rebates a standard .27% for all slot and video poker machines. Every Wednesday is double-point day. The machine selection (as well as blackjack) is among the best in Laughlin. Video poker players can choose from quarter full-pay deuces and 9/6 jacks, or dollar 9/6 jacks and 10/7 double bonus. *Recommended.*

Note: If you're not already a member of Harrah's Las Vegas slot club, get your card in Laughlin so you can flash it in Las Vegas to get free show tickets.

Pioneer Hotel & Casino - All-American Round-Up Club

Owned by Sahara Gaming, the Pioneer hotel rooms are rather rustic, but the grub ain't bad, especially at Granny's, its ultra-classy gourmet room, one of the best restaurants in Nevada. The multi-level slot club has a base cash rebate of .33% for slots and .17% for video poker, but with double-point days (several each month) and point bonuses awarded at each level, you can easily triple both percentages. The Round-up Club is also generous with food and meal comps. Video poker players will find full-pay deuces and 9/6 jacks at the quarter level, and 9/6 jacks for dollar play. *Recommended.*

Ramada Express Hotel & Casino - Slot Club

Located on the west side of the strip away from the river, this first-class resort towers over Laughlin. Though the club has a low cash rebate (less than .20% for slots and .05% for video poker), double and triple times are offered every week. Once you obtain 200 points (approximately $750 coin-in for slots, $2,000 for video poker), you qualify for a casino rate of $14 Sunday through Friday. New members getting 500 points within 48 hours earn two free nights. The casino has several quarter and dollar 9/6 jacks paying 375 coins for 7777 (100.42% average payback without the slot club). *Recommended.*

MESQUITE

Many Las Vegas and Utah locals go to Mesquite for a quick getaway. The three resort properties (Oasis does not have a slot club yet) are inexpensive, friendly, and offer many amenities, including golf. Located about a half-hour north (on the top of the Virgin River Gorge) is St. George, Utah, with an impressive Mormon temple and one of the country's best outlet shopping centers.

Player's Island Resort - Player's Preferred Club

Merv Griffin's Atlantic City background comes through a little too loud and clear at his new resort in Mesquite. The design is attractive, but both the slot club and machine inventory are so-so. The Player's Preferred Club does not pay cash. Points must be redeemed for meals or logoed items, for an average return of .50%. Machine selection, especially at the quarter level, is poor. There are a few dollar 9/6 jacks.

Virgin River Hotel & Casino - Royalty Card

Originally a gambling stop for truckers, the Virgin River has grown to 379 rooms. The hotel offers several extras including a pool and a four-screen movie theater. Meals here are well priced, especially the buffet.

The new club is a "don't ask, won't tell" secretive system. Also, the operation appeared to be understaffed. The casino offers quarter full-pay deuces and 9/6 jacks, as well as dollar 9/6 jacks.

Ratings Roster

Caesars Palace	*Emperors Club*	★★★1/2
Desert Inn	*Celebrity Club*	★★★1/2
Four Queens	*Reel Winners Club*	★★★1/2
Golden Nugget	*24 Karat Club*	★★★1/2
Sam's Town	*Town Club*	★★★1/2
San Remo	*Money Club*	★★★1/2
Treasure Island	*Treasure Island Club*	★★★
Flamingo	*Flamingo Player's Club*	★★★
Lady Luck	*Mad Money Club*	★★★
Mirage	*Club Mirage*	★★★
Boomtown	*Player's Club*	★★★
Fiesta	*Amigo Club*	★★★
Frontier	*Gold Rush Club*	★★★
Rio	*Play Rio*	★★★
Sahara	*Preferred Gold Card*	★★★
Santa Fe	*Player's Edge*	★★★
California	*Cal Club*	★★1/2
Gold Coast	*The Club*	★★1/2
Stardust	*Stardust Slot Club*	★★1/2
Barbary Coast	*Fun Club*	★★1/2
Circus Circus	*Ringmaster Club*	★★1/2
Excalibur	*Crown Club*	★★1/2
Fremont	*Five Star Slot Club*	★★1/2
Hacienda	*Club Viva*	★★1/2
Las Vegas Hilton	*Club Magic*	★★1/2
Riviera	*Gold Club*	★★1/2
Showboat	*Officer's Club*	★★1/2
Tom's Sunset	*Slot Seeker's Club*	★★1/2
Westward Ho	*Preferred Customer Card*	★★1/2
Harrah's	*Gold Card*	★★
Luxor	*Gold Chamber*	★★
Texas	*Player's Club*	★★
Tropicana	*Island Winner's Club*	★★
Hard Rock	*Back Stage Pass*	★★
Jerry's Nugget	*More Club*	★★
MGM Grand	*MGM Player's Club*	★★
Sands	*Sandsational Slot Club*	★★
Bally's	*MVP Club*	★1/2
Imperial Palace	*Imperial Player's Club*	★1/2
Nevada Palace	*Player's Circle*	★1/2

Casinos and Their Slot Clubs

Note: References in boldface indicate individual reviews.

Las Vegas, North Las Vegas, and Henderson

Aladdin—*Prestige Membership Club* 17, 59, **63**
Bally's—*MVP Club* 3, 48, 57, **64**
Barbary Coast—*Fun Club* 12, 21, 23, 26, 41, 55, 57, **65**
Boomtown—*Player's Club* 26, 56, 57, **66**
Boulder Station—*Boarding Pass* 7, 55, 57, 59, **67**, 101
Caesars Palace—*Emperors Club* 2, 3, 4, 11, 46, 48, 53, 55, 56,
     57, 58, 59, 64, **68**
California—*Cal Club* 40, 57, **69**
Circus Circus—*Ringmaster Club* 17, 42, **70**
Desert Inn—*Celebrity Club* 9, 40, 52, 55, 56, 57, 58, **71**
Excalibur—*Crown Club* 2, 18, 55, 57, **72**
Fiesta—*Amigo Club* 4, 27, 55, 57, **73**
Flamingo—*Flamingo Player's Club* 53, 55, 57, **74**
Four Queens—*Reel Winners Club* 23, 40, 43, 46, 48, 49, 52, 54,
     57, 58, **75**
Fremont—*Five Star Slot Club* 48, 54, 57, **76**
Frontier—*Gold Rush Club* 13, 19, 21, 23, 26, 46, 51, 52, 57,
     58, **77**
Gold Coast—*The Club* 7, 8, 22, 23, 28, 42, 56, 57, 65, **78**
Golden Nugget—*24 Karat Club* 1, 2, 3, 5, 12, 26, 40, 43, 55, 57,
     58, **79**, 89
Hacienda—*Club Viva* 4, 46, **80**
Hard Rock—*Back Stage Pass* 9, 17, 27, 57, **81**
Harrah's—*Gold Card* 8, **82**, 109
Imperial Palace—*Imperial Player's Club* 9, 57, **83**
Jerry's Nugget—*More Club* 23, 57, **84**

Index

About the Author

At the age of nine, Jeffrey Compton learned poker and pinochle from his mother. He has been fascinated by cards, casinos, and gambling ever since. While the owner of an industrial manufacturing and distribution company in Ohio, he organized and managed Cleveland's largest and most elegant casino night annually for twelve years. Now a Las Vegas resident, Compton regularly contributes to the *Las Vegas Advisor*, the *Grogan Casino Report*, and Stanford Wong's *Current Blackjack News*. At last count, he was a member of 75 slot clubs.

Subscribe to the Las Vegas Advisor and get in on a local secret!

Five reasons to read the Advisor...

Here's what Las Vegas Advisor subscribers are saying:

"I get more of the kind of money saving information I need by reading the Las Vegas Advisor than I receive from local papers and TV combined."

"We're regular LVA subscribers, and when we come to Vegas to visit our relatives, we know more about Las Vegas than they do!"

1 VALUE. The *Advisor* finds it. You benefit from it. Get more for less. Every month, the Top Ten Values let you in on the best deals.

2 PROFITABILITY. The *Advisor* provides you with $300 worth of money saving coupons (no out-of-state ID required) for buffets, fine dining, shows, matchplay, slot & video poker bonuses and free plays, and much, much, more.

3 CONVENIENCE. This 12-page newsletter (no ads) is your one-stop resource for what's new and hot going on in Las Vegas. Dining, gambling, entertainment, news, promotions, best values. Concise, comprehensive and fun to have along.

4 INSIDE TRACK. The *Advisor* reveals who's doing what, where, when, how, and why you should (or should not) partake.

5 INFORMATION. Our staff of crack researchers comb the city looking for the best deals available and pass them on to you.

With the Las Vegas Advisor, you get more out of Las Vegas than Las Vegas gets out of you!

Huntington Press

5280 S. Valley View Blvd., Suite B • Las Vegas, Nevada • 89118
Phone: (800) 244-2224 • Fax: (702) 597-5208 • E-mail: lva@infi.net

YES! I want to buy a subscription to the Las Vegas Advisor!

☐ I am enclosing $45 for one year of the LVA plus a FREE Reference Guide and a Las Vegas Advisor Subscriber Benefit Package (worth over $300!). NV residents must add 7% sales tax.

I am paying by: ☐ check/money order   ☐ Visa/MasterCard/Discover

Account # _____ Exp. _____

Signature _____ Phone _____

Name _____

Address _____

City _____ State _____ Zip _____

Look for these Huntington Press

Bargain City:
Booking, Betting, and Beating the New Las Vegas
by Anthony Curtis

Las Vegas is rapidly changing, and locals and visitors alike are reaping the benefits, thanks to *Bargain City*. This 238-page bargain-packed book chronicles a decade's worth of Las Vegas changes, focusing on the values and gambling opportunities that have made Las Vegas America's number-one place to play.

Bargain City is not a typical guide to Las Vegas. It is a meticulously detailed consumer directory for value-conscious visitors (and locals) to the discount capital of the world.

238 pages   soft cover $11.95   ISBN # 0-929712-50-1

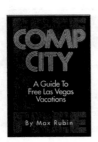

Comp City: A Guide to Free Las Vegas Vacations
by Max Rubin

The premise is simple: most casinos dangle complimentaries in front of players to get a shot at their bankrolls. In his groundbreaking book, *Comp City: A Guide to Free Las Vegas Vacations*, Max Rubin shows players how to dangle their bankrolls to lure the casino's complimentaries.

The casino comp system is designed to encourage and reward gamblers by giving them back 40¢ in comps for every $1 they lose by gambling. Rubin turns the tables on the gambling joints by disclosing a method for getting $1 worth of comps for every 10¢-30¢ in casino losses. The system entails beating the casinos with a combination of gambling savvy, camouflage, and thorough insider's understanding of how the system works. Includes a chapter for "locals only."

296 pages   hard cover $39.95   ISBN 0-929712-35-8

books at your local bookstore:

Theory of Blackjack:
The Compleat Card Counters
Guide to the Casino Game of 21
by Peter Griffin

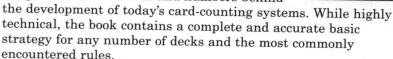

The bible for serious players. Griffin's classic
work on the mathematics of blackjack provides
insight into the methods and numbers behind
the development of today's card-counting systems. While highly
technical, the book contains a complete and accurate basic
strategy for any number of decks and the most commonly
encountered rules.

"*The Theory of Blackjack* is a fundamental contribution to
our understanding of the game ... unusually well written and
amusing ... a pleasure to read."

—Ed Thorp, author of *Beat the Dealer*

254 pages   soft cover $9.95   ISBN 0-915141-02-7

Extra Stuff:
Gambling Ramblings
by Peter Griffin

Math-master Griffin delves deeply into gambling in this compilation of his most famous
magazine articles and conference papers, which
include his famous "Mathematical Expectation
for the Public's Play in Casino Blackjack."
Griffin's style accommodates most readers,
regardless of mathematical expertise or gambling experience.

170 pages   soft cover $11.95   ISBN 9-929712-00

Also available directly from the publisher.
Call 1 (800) 244-2224

Be the first to know!

*Call 1 (800) 244-2224
and ask to be put on the
Huntington Press mailing list.*

Receive advance notice of:
- New products
- Special offers
- Book signings